THE
CONSCIOUS
AND
COURAGEOUS
LEADER

THE
CONSCIOUS
AND
COURAGEOUS
LEADER

DEVELOPING YOUR AUTHENTIC VOICE
TO LEAD AND INSPIRE

DR. TRACY TOMASKY

DEDICATION

This book is dedicated to:

Alina, with gratitude for your unconditional love and endless belief in me.
You are the ever-present sunrise in my life.

Amelia, you have found your courageous to create the life of your dreams.
Keep shining your light to illuminate your own path and inspire others.

Conscious and courageous leaders who inspire us all to discover
our highest good.

ACKNOWLEDGEMENTS

WRITING THIS BOOK involved so much more than the words that ended up on the pages. For me, it was the reflections on the journey of my life that spoke as I wrote each chapter. My editor encouraged me to get personal, tell stories, and share my real-world experiences. As I followed her guidance, my heart opened, and I found myself feeling vulnerable. I gathered my courage to get out of my own way and embrace the feeling. The process was yet another opportunity for me to follow what I coach others to do and walk my talk.

There were so many colleagues and friends who supported me all the way through this process. Heartfelt thanks to Dr. Jody Graf, Karen Finley, Vera Vaccarro, Linda Martin, Dr. Tamra Taylor, Steve Enoch, Denise Lee, Faye Diskin, Anya Clasen, Mala Ahuja, Roxanne Gustitus, Kathy Kukrall, Christine Mattos, Desi Soto, Dr. Kevin Peters, Denice Peterson, Nancy Haas, Julian Haas, Donna Sneeringer, Dr. Linda Petty, Dr. Ellen Rosen, Estelle Jones, Alison Kimmel, Sean Deegan, Ed and Pat Lapointe.

I am ever grateful to Alicia Dunams, (founder of Bestseller in a Weekend) my business coach and motivator who encouraged me to be courageous and continually push the boundaries of my comfort zone. I couldn't have asked for a more competent, inspiring, and engaged coach. Her team, especially Toccara Ross, was there to guide me every step of the way. If you are thinking of writing a book and want coaching from the best, I give Alicia Dunams my highest recommendation. www.AliciaDunams.com

A big thank you to my clients, who I am blessed to serve. I treasure your trust in yourself and in me to walk beside you on your leadership journey. What you have taught me is invaluable.

Heartfelt gratitude to all of my ECE friends and colleagues. Our time together was filled with every emotion possible over the decades we've spent together. You have taught and inspired me, and you will live in my heart always.

Finally, I want to acknowledge Gloria Partida, founder of the Davis Phoenix Coalition. I am inspired by the strength and courage that guided you to rise from a horrific experience to create and lead an organization that works to ensure that all people are safe, respected, and free from violence. You serve your mission tirelessly, and it is my honor to serve with you. **www.davisphoenixco.org**

TABLE OF CONTENTS

INTRODUCTION

What lies behind us and what lies before us are tiny matters compared to what lies within us.

– Ralph Waldo Emerson

WHO IS A conscious and courageous leader? I am. You are. I believe that in the deepest part of all of us is a conscious and courageous leader, whether we are the CEO of a large organization, a PTA President, the leader of our family, or the leader of our self. Being conscious, knowing there is something bigger than ourselves and being courageous, acting beyond our comfort zone, are abilities deep within us. Finding the key to unlock that core wisdom is what this book is about.

Having more than 20 years of experience in leadership roles and owning my own business, coaching leaders, I have experienced firsthand the complexity and immense responsibilities that leaders face. I have also experienced the other side of leadership, which is the opportunity to influence and make positive changes in organizations and communities. While leadership positions can offer power, prestige, and a higher paycheck, most leaders I've worked with are motivated by the difference they can make in their organization. Whatever the reason, once the excitement of being chosen as the leader wears off, the real world of being a leader sets in and trepidation ensues. New leaders face challenges they haven't encountered before, and they haven't developed the skills to address those complicated situations. I have seen too many leaders selected for their position with an expectation that they already know how to fulfill their role or they will just somehow figure it out. Their supervisors are too busy to coach or train them, which leaves many leaders to fend for themselves. The phone calls I get from my clients have a similar ring: How do I deal with these difficult people? How do I make decisions that don't create hostility? How do I manage priorities when everything is a priority? I'm working so many hours that I don't have time for my family or a life outside of my work, and I'm tired!

My clients are dedicated, passionate, and committed to their work; they want to be the best leaders they can be. The common denominator when they struggle, however, can be condensed to three basic areas: knowing the deeper part of themselves and their core values, and the ability to apply them to decision making, skills needed for successful interpersonal interactions, and a personal wellness plan for taking care of themselves. From my own experience as a leader and in observing hundreds of other leaders, I believe that core values, authenticity, communication, relationships, and personal wellness make up the foundation for strong leadership. With a strong foundation in place, leaders are poised to develop the other skills they'll need to lead successfully.

This book covers these five foundational elements and provides the information and strategies to help leaders as they discover, develop, improve, and apply them in their leadership role.

This book will enable you, as a leader, to gain the ability to clarify your priorities and improve your ability to make decisions. You will learn what it means to be authentic and how to develop your authenticity. You will uncover your beliefs and the core values that have been driving your life and will learn strategies to effectively communicate your message, as well as strategies to diffuse and resolve conflict. You will learn how to harness the power of relationships and how to create and maintain a balanced lifestyle to have greater stamina and strong mental focus. And you will experience the benefits of self-reflection, the key to creating the life that you want.

By reading this book and engaging in the material, you will learn how to develop a solid foundation of who you are before you begin to manage others, whether you are a new or experienced leader.

Leadership and Courage

"Courage is what it takes to stand up and speak; courage is also what it takes to sit down and listen."

– Winston Churchill

We often associate courage with heroic acts or spontaneous reactions that are bigger than life: the person who runs into a burning building to rescue someone trapped inside, a shop owner who charges a robber holding a gun and thwarts a holdup, a jogger who hears screams coming from the lake and dives in to save a drowning victim. When these heroic people are honored, they are often asked where they found the courage to be so brave. A common thread in their response is, "It wasn't anything extraordinary; I just did what I had to do in the moment. Anyone would have done the same." They were just doing what they had to do. To the hero, courage is not a choice, but a voice inside them that says, "I must."

I've had the privilege of working with and learning from a few very courageous people. In my personal world, however, my own hero who wears the badge of courage is Nancy, my sister. Nancy was the third oldest of five children, and I was the "baby," as they called me. As I was growing up, I admired Nancy's adventurous spirit. She was the only sibling lucky enough to have her own horse, and she worked tirelessly taking care of it and riding it in horse shows. Nancy was always brave and traveled by herself to Germany right after high school and to Taiwan a year later. She learned to speak German and Taiwanese and immersed herself in each culture. Her passion for life and caring for others led her to pursue a career in teaching; and for the next 40 years, she taught essential life skills to high school students. Just a year after she retired, Nancy was diagnosed with cancer, not once, but three times over the next four years. With each diagnosis, she let herself feel the deep dread, but only briefly. She knew the following weeks would bring a difficult course of harsh treatments, but she made a choice each time. Nancy chose to be courageous. She had the courage to not give in to the fear of what the diagnosis could possibly bring, but rather walked right through the fear to focus on what was most important to her: her family, friends, and animals. Throughout her treatments, Nancy would wake up early every morning, move through the pain and walk down to her barn to feed her horses and the stray cats who took up residence there. During the middle of one chemo series, she worked with her oncologist to adjust the treatments so she could accompany her husband on a trip they had planned to Nepal. She embraced everything about that trip, visiting with the people in the villages and joining them in their dance celebrations, with her bald head and all! Nancy is the embodiment of courage at its finest.

Sibling note: My oldest sister, Susanne, is another story of courage; however, her life is a whole book in itself!

Courage and leadership go hand in hand. The most successful leaders must call upon courage at a moment's notice, whether it's facing an angry customer, standing by an unpopular decision, having difficult conversations with employees, terminating an employee, responding to an unfavorable review finding, or speaking truth to power.

I have experienced all of these difficult scenarios and more. Early in my career as a leader, I would come home upset because someone would inevitably be very unhappy with a decision I made. It seemed like I could never please everyone. It took a while to finally realize that not only would I never please everyone, but if I was pleasing everyone, it meant I was playing it safe and not making the best decisions. It took courage for me to be transparent about decisions I made and be open to listening to feedback, favorable or not. But it also took courage to listen to feedback and change the course of a decision, if that was best for the organization. Ego sometimes wants to get in our way of being able to change decisions. Whenever I felt my ego getting in my way, I gathered my courage and stayed true to my commitment to be my best self, which helped my ego take a back seat.

As a leader, I've been in countless conversations that have been difficult. I've expressed unpopular opinions to superintendents, school boards, executive teams, and unions. Each time a situation needed to be challenged, I mustered up my courage and followed my core value of commitment to the truth. I often felt like the little boy in Hans Christian Andersen's story, *The Emperor's New Clothes*, being the only one willing or brave enough to call out an obvious truth. What I observed during those times was that others saw what I saw, but they didn't use their courage to stand up and be heard. They let fear take charge, which stunned them into silence. I'm not saying it was always easy to speak truth to power. There were times that my insides were shaking or my voice quivered, and being courageous was often a lonely path. For me, that's where being conscious steps in. My conscience guides my ethics, and the courage deep within me seems to say, "You must, and I will give you strength to speak your truth." I have learned to trust my inner voice.

I believe everyone has the ability to be courageous. Courage lives in each of us; we just need to develop the skills to allow it to show itself. More simply put, courage is expressed by going out of your comfort zone. It is about broadening your boundary of security so you establish a wider comfort zone with each effort.

The strategies that help you learn to develop your courage are similar to strategies that help you become more comfortable with change. Everyone is different; what requires courage for some may be easy for others. If courage seems like a scary prospect to you, begin by getting out of your comfort zone in small steps.

Following are a few specific strategies to stretch your comfort zone:

- Take a different route to work tomorrow.
- Spend your lunch hour in a totally new way.
- Volunteer to do something you normally would not agree to.
- The next time you're in a restaurant, order something you've never had before.
- Force yourself to say "no" to at least one request this week.
- Ask somebody that question you've always wanted to ask him or her.
- Express an opinion that may be unpopular.
- Speak in front of a group – start with a small group.

Courage is a powerful tool for every leader to have. Courage transcends the moment. Courage lives inside of you and through your action is made known. It is your internal voice that expresses itself without hesitation.

Courage lives in you; activate it and make a powerful impact!

My Trail of Courage

Courage began to show itself early in my life and has continued to be a significant part of my leadership character throughout my career. I've chosen a few key moments to illustrate the role courage has played in my life and have included them in each chapter. Building your courage can start slowly, from writing a letter, to questioning a decision, to advocating your point, and speaking truth to power. As you read my experiences, take time to reflect on your own life and times when you have exemplified courage, too.

Leader of Leaders

As the president of an Administrators Association, it was my job to represent the voice of about 75 of my colleagues. When an agreement that the Association had made with the previous superintendent was about to expire, it was my job to get the new superintendent to renew it for another year. The new superintendent was not in favor of this agreement, and I knew it would not be an easy road. In meeting after meeting, he would entertain the discussion with me, but it didn't seem likely that he would sign it. With the responsibility of being the president and the weight of my colleagues on my shoulders, I had to muster the courage to continue bringing the issue forward. My consistent effort and courage paid off as the superintendent eventually did sign the agreement. Along with finding my courage, it was the relationship and trust I had built with this superintendent over time that led to that success.

Point of Courage: Fulfilling the role of being a leader and representing the voice of those I led, bringing a tough issue forward, and advocating for it to an authority figure.

How to Use This Book

This book is designed to help you develop the leadership tools you are seeking. By reading this book and completing the exercises, you have chosen a path, a journey into yourself. As a leader, this deeper learning will yield the kind of results that will inspire those around you.

Doing the Reflection Activities and Assessments

To get the best results from doing the reflections and assessments in this book, set aside a block of uninterrupted time and find a quiet space to call your own. The time that you are investing is a gift to yourself.

Go slow; you know yourself best—you can read though the chapter first and then go back and do the exercises or complete the reflections as you read, whichever way is most meaningful to you.

Reflect without judgment; step back and take a balcony view and observe yourself. If you discover something about yourself that prompts self-criticism, replace that thought with a non-judgmental point of view. Switch "I'm so inept," with "Isn't that interesting." By being an observer, rather than a critical judge, you give yourself space to breathe. In that space, learn to marvel at and appreciate everything that brought you to where you are in that moment. You are whole and perfect. Let that in. . .

Embarking on an inward journey may trigger an unpleasant memory at times, so it is important to have support available. You may want to journal your thoughts and feelings or have a friend or professional ready to talk with.

Being a Conscious and Courageous Leader

You have chosen to answer a very important call, to be a leader. Having made that choice reflects the courage you already have inside of you. Being a leader is not an easy endeavor, and at times you may not be the favorite person in the room. You will face adversity and challenge. You will have the power to influence, change, and steer the direction of the organization you lead. To be an effective leader is to be courageous.

Being a conscious leader is about self-awareness and letting go of judgment, criticism, and the need to be right. A conscious leader is someone who knows they are serving a greater purpose to make the world a better place. It's about ethics and integrity to honor the core values that reflect your goodness.

Our world needs leaders who are conscious and courageous to help lift and inspire everyone to activate their own gifts and talents for the greater good.

This book and my Leadership Development Reflection System in Chapter Six were written and designed to be ongoing tools to help you grow your leadership skills.

With humble appreciation, I thank you for reading this book and wish you all the best on your leadership journey!

Tracy

Chapter One

THE POWER OF KNOWING
YOUR VALUES AND BELIEFS

*"Your beliefs become your thoughts. Your thoughts become your words.
Your words become your actions. Your actions become your habits.
Your habits become your values. Your values become your destiny."*

– Mahatma Gandhi

GROWING UP IN a small town in PA, the words "beliefs"
and "values" weren't talked about, but were dictated as
a cemented way of living. Everyone knew the "right way" to
live their life. I attended the local Catholic school from first
through fourth grade and quickly learned how I was supposed
to respond to authority, with absolute deference and non-
questioning respect. Those were the days when hitting students
was a normal part of discipline, and I unfortunately experienced
my share of feeling the sting of a wooden ruler with a metal
edge. The exuberant learning spirit I entered school with was
challenged repeatedly as the questions I wanted to voice were
silenced … temporarily.

When I was in the second grade, the local bishop came to
visit our school. I was impressed with his elaborate "uniform"
and commanding presence. In my excitement to meet him,
I forgot the demure approach I was expected to show. I was
captivated by the large ring he had on his hand and gushed
about how beautiful it was. Unlike the nuns who taught me, he
welcomed my enthusiasm and questions. He took off his ring
and let me try it on. I was so proud to show everyone around

me ... until I caught the glare of Sister Mary Catherine (not her real name) across the room. I quickly gave the ring back to the bishop. Later that afternoon, I was admonished for being so disrespectful to actually put on this holy ring. I responded, "But he gave it to me to put on." That was apparently not the response she was looking for and out came that dreaded ruler once again. So began the installation of my beliefs and core values toward authority.

From those and other similar early experiences:

My Belief: Authority is all-powerful. Don't question authority; and if you do, there will be a price to pay.

My Learned Value: Authority in the context of reverence

The story above accounts for one set of experiences that shaped my early thinking and believing. It illustrates how during those early years, before age 7, we accept what comes to us as true and begin to develop our beliefs and foundational values. The good news – our values and beliefs are not "cemented in stone;" we get to decide what we believe and how those beliefs inform our values. I am happy to say that over time, through new experiences and intentional focus and by using some of the exercises I share with you in this book, I have transformed that particular belief and value related to authority.

My Current Belief: Authority is a position of power, and it is essential that anyone in a position of power uses it respectfully. Questioning authority or speaking truth to power, when done with integrity and respect, can lead to a better decision, practice, or product.

My Current Value: Authority in the context of responsibility and accountability

Following is another example of how my early years formed my beliefs and values. Close to my home was a magical forest. We called it "the woods," but I call it magical because I spent unending hours there as an explorer going on great adventures through far-away lands, as a warrior with my bow and arrows, keeping all the living things safe. Yes, I did actually have a little red bow and set of arrows in a small leather quiver that I proudly wore on my little seven-year-old body. I was in my own world in the woods, a world where I was connected to all of the living things. I had many conversations with those trees, squirrels, bunnies, and birds. I learned to listen deep inside of myself and learned to trust my inner voice.

From those experiences:
My Belief:
Nature is healing, energizing, and a great place to visit my inner self.
My inner voice informs my truth.

My Learned Value:
Nature is a respite.
I value my inner voice and use it as my compass.
My current beliefs and values related to nature and my inner voice have remained an integral part of who I am today. I access them when I need to make decisions or find a quiet place to listen to my inner guidance.

VALUES AND BELIEFS

What are Values and Beliefs?

Beliefs are our convictions, what we know to be true. They are thoughts that we keep thinking over and over again. Our beliefs create our reality, and what we believe, we become.

Here is an example of how an experience early on helped me develop a powerful belief:

> In the fifth grade, I transferred to our local public school and was blessed to have an amazing teacher, Mrs. Horst. She was kind, caring, and she always inspired us to do our best work. During her class, we had a creative writing period; and she actually took us into the woods behind our school and had each of us find a special creative writing place. I found a perfect nook in the crook of a comfortable old tree. I remember one particular creative writing session. I had read *Jonathon Livingston Seagull* and reflected on a quote from that book, "They can because they think they can." My world began to change. A whole new way "to be" opened up for me as I integrated the modeling of kindness, caring, and excellence I learned from Mrs. Horst, and the endless possibilities knowing "I can if I think I can." That particular belief is still anchored to my core to this day. I believe I can, so I do!

A value is our sense of right and wrong, our standard of how we live our life. Hyrum Smith defines values as *"… what we believe to be of greatest importance and the highest priority in our lives."*

Values cover all areas of our lives: health, career, finances, and relationships. Core values are those values that are most significant to you. These core values create a foundation for decision-making that is aligned with your mind and spirit.

Where Do Values and Beliefs Come From, and How are They Developed?

As in the examples I provided at the beginning of this chapter, beliefs and values come from many sources: our schools, our environment while growing up, our friends, teachers, parents, siblings, neighbors, culture, media, and significant emotional events. All sources of interaction and input form and establish our values and beliefs.

Values are developed in stages. Sociologist Morris Massey describes the periods of development in ages 0-21.

Ages 0-7 is our imprint period—a person at this age doesn't have judgments or filters and accepts what comes to them as being true.

Ages 7-14 is our modeling period – someone at this age now has conscious thinking and models who/what they see.

Ages 14-21 is our socialization period – in this stage, we like people who are like us and group ourselves with those who are similar to ourselves.

After age 21, we move into our adult roles and responsibilities. As we mature, we grow into our beliefs, and as our lives change, we can respond to those changes. While there is a sequence of development for our growth, both beliefs and values can change if they no longer serve us.

If you desire to change a belief, follow these steps:

- surface an awareness of the belief
- challenge it and explore its impact on you
- shift your focus to what you want it to be
- reinforce your new thinking every time the belief arises

Examples:

1. If the message from growing up with a belief around money was "Money doesn't grow on trees," or "You have to work hard for your money" -

   The learned belief/value as a result: I struggle to make money because I believe it is hard. Or, I am extremely frugal because money doesn't grow on trees.

   Changing the belief: Believing in abundance and coming back into balance, knowing the belief in "lack" was an unnecessary fear that no longer serves you.

2. If your parents worked long hours, missed family events because of work, and weren't able to be present with you when they were at home -

    The learned belief/value as a result: Work is more important than anything, including me.

    Changing the belief: I am important; my family is important. Work is not my identity; it is my vocation, only one part of who I am.

Why are Values and Beliefs Important for Leaders?

Leaders see the people they lead through the lens of their beliefs and values. Our beliefs create our reality, or as Anais Nin said, "We don't see the world as it is, but as we are." Our reactions, our decisions, and how we set priorities are all influenced by our beliefs and values.

> *"Values and beliefs are the compass that informs a leader's direction."*
>
> – Tracy Tomasky

Leaders experience complex and demanding situations every day. There are competing demands for their priorities, so they, and the people they manage, often end up in a spiral of "everything is priority." The result of this confusion and lack of focus is that both the leaders and their staffs feel frustrated.

I experienced the "spiral of priorities" phenomenon firsthand when I was the director of a large department that served over 4,000 children and families and employed 350 staff members. Our programs were governed by as many as 14 different funding sources, all with their own unique guidelines and mandates. When I first stepped into the leadership role, I got caught up in "everything's priority," and that is what I conveyed to my staff. My decision making was inconsistent and lead to my exceptionally competent and committed staff members being frustrated. I was frustrated, too.

Here is where beliefs and values enter the picture. I knew I had to do something different, beyond just learning how to prioritize better. Prioritizing was only part of the issue. I did what life had taught me—I sought out a quiet space and asked myself for guidance. I listened. It became very clear to me as my values around relationships, excellence, and integrity came into focus.

My value of integrity told me to base my decisions on what was best for the children and families we served.

My values around relationships had me rethink the effect of "everything's priority" on my staff. I believed it was important for me to treat people as people first and workers second. By expecting an impossible result of making everything priority, I was not honoring my staff as people, but rather treating them more like robots. I cringe when thinking of those times; however, acknowledging my core value of relationships forced me to find other solutions.

Finally, my value of excellence helped me lead in a way that expected and applauded best effort when focused on results. I believe in excellence, not perfection. Perfection causes stress; excellence produces quality work that inspires more of the same. The staff was creative and willing to take chances and risks in new approaches, because I believe they felt safe to do so.

When you are aware of and aligned with your core values, it becomes your foundation. You will have a center for future action based on a foundation of values. Another benefit of being clear on your core values is that you will be able to find a respite in yourself. You will always have a retreat to go to anytime you want. For leaders, this place of calm and centering is invaluable.

Discovering Your Core Values

As you embark on this journey to discover your own core values, take time to reflect on what is important to you. The following five-step process will help you reflect at a deep level and uncover where your beliefs and values came from, and give you an opportunity to decide if they are currently the beliefs and values that guide you to be the best leader you can and want to be.

Reflection Activity #1

Think back to your youngest years, between the ages of 0-7. What messages did you receive in the following areas?

Health:

Work:

Family:

Spirituality/Religion:

Money:

Think about the people who positively influenced you during this time. What qualities did they have that you respected or looked up to?

Move forward in time reflecting on ages 7-14. Were those messages the same, or did they change? If they did change, how so?

Think about the people who positively influenced you during this time. What qualities did they have that you respected or looked up to?

Move forward in time, now reflecting on ages 14-21. Were those messages the same, or did they change? If they did change, how so?

Think about the people who positively influenced you during this time. What qualities did they have that you respected or looked up to?

Move forward in time, reflecting on ages 21+. How are those messages being reflected in your life?

Think about the people who positively influenced you during this time. What qualities did they have that you respected or looked up to?

What are your key learnings from this reflection?

Reflection Activity #2

Discovering Your Values

Our values are what we place the highest priority on in our lives. Values influence the choices and decisions we make. Think about what is most important to you and reflect on the questions below to help you in the process of naming your values.

What gets you excited? What do you enjoy doing in your free time?

What issues are you willing to stand up and be heard about?

What boundaries do you have that are non-negotiable?

What's on your list of things that you will do "someday?"

When your life is over, what do you want to be remembered for?

Reflection Activity #3

Circle 15-20 words from the list below that represent the values that are most important to you.

Acceptance	Accomplishment	Achievement
Accountability	Adaptability	Authenticity
Authority	Belonging	Career
Commitment	Community	Competition
Cooperation	Contribution	Courage
Creativity	Curiosity	Challenge
Compassion	Development	Diversity
Effort	Empathy	Excellence
Faith	Family	Freedom
Friends	Financial security	Fun

Generosity   Humility   Harmony
Individuality   Innovation   Integrity
Justice   Kindness   Knowledge
Love   Learning   Loyalty
Organization   Peace   Personal Growth
Recreation   Reflection   Relationships
Relaxation   Respect   Risk taking
Self-awareness   Self-Reliance   Sense of humor
Service   Solitude   Spiritual alignment
Success   Truth   Wellness
Work/Life Balance Other:_____   _____

Reflection Activity #4

Determining Your Top Three Core Values

Using the words you circled from the values list, group together the values that have a similar meaning to you into three groups. For each of the three groups, choose a unifying word that represents the meaning of the entire group. Your unifying word may be one of the words on the list or choose a different word. These unifying words represent the three values that are most important to you.

Group 1:   Group 2:   Group 3:

_____   _____   _____

_____   _____   _____

_____   _____   _____

_____   _____   _____

_____   _____   _____

_____   _____   _____

Unifying Word: Unifying Word: Unifying Word:

_____   _____   _____

My top three values are:

_____   _____   _____

Reflection Activity #5

Personal Signature Statement

A signature statement is a concrete way of distilling all of your values together. It's the deep reflective work of what those values look like in your life and how you're applying them in your life's mission. Your signature statement is your personal mission statement.

My signature statement that represents my top three values of truth, service, and learning is:

"I am open to new learning and live my truth to contribute to a world where every living thing is valued. I help leaders awaken to themselves and their capabilities, find their authentic voice, and express it respectfully and effectively. I use my leadership skills to serve and advocate for social justice."

Creating a personal signature statement is a powerful way to integrate your top three values to reflect your core values. Just like all values, your personal signature statement may change over time. As you grow and evolve, priorities shift and new core values may emerge.

Step 1.

Review your top three values and reflect on where you see evidence of each value in your life. One value may have priority over another; however, given the complexity of real-life scenarios, there will be times when your priorities among your top three core values will shift.

Step 2.

From your reflections in steps 1-4, write your personal signature statement. Include all three core values in your personal signature statement. To help you get started, sample statement templates are listed below. You may use one of these formats or create a format of your own.

Sample Formats:

I am committed to living each day with… (value), so that… (what living by these values will give you). I will do this by… (specific behaviors you will use to live these values).

I resolve to… (be or do)… so that… (reason why this is important). I will do this by… (specific behaviors that will get you there).

Examples:

Top three core values: Relationships, Authenticity, Creativity

I am committed to living life authentically in relationship with others to empower mine and their creative expression and growth. I will share openly with others, encourage them to do the same, and listen without judgment.

Top three core values: Self-Reliance, Trustworthy, Adventurous

I live each day being self-sufficient, honest, and courageous so that I will be fulfilled, joyful, and at peace in my world. I will do this by taking time to be thoughtful and thankful and seeking out new experiences with family and friends.

My Personal Signature Statement

_____

_____

_____

_____

_____

_____

Applying Your Core Values to Decision-making:

Now that you have determined your own core values and have written your Personal Signature Statement, use them as the lens through which you view the following scenarios. How would you use your core values to respond to the following scenarios?

- Scenario: Your boss asks you to stay late for the third night in a row. You haven't spent time with your family all week. What values do you check in with to make this decision?

- Scenario: Your parent who lives a plane ride away from you is sick. You can easily afford the plane ticket. Your spouse can stay home and take care of the children. Your boss is not happy that you will be missing work. What do you do?

- Scenario: You basically work paycheck to paycheck to pay your bills. You get a bonus one month. Do you save the money? Do you donate the money? Do you spend the money?

- Scenario: Your 10-year-old son is asking for a new bike. You have the money to easily buy him a new bike. Do you buy him a new bike? Do you have him help contribute to buying a new bike?

- Scenario: You are the leader of a small organization. The workload is high for your employees. One of your employees comes to you and says she has a family emergency and needs to be gone for two weeks. What values do you check in with to make this decision?

- Scenario: As the leader of your organization, you have an opportunity to bring in a large contract that will yield significant income for the company. The contract is with someone known for overcharging customers for inferior products. What values do you check in with to make this decision?

- Scenario: Being healthy is a core value for you. You have been running from meeting to meeting all day long; you haven't taken a break or eaten since you left home that morning. It's 1 o'clock. You have 30 minutes before your next meeting. You haven't checked your email or returned any phone calls that day. A disgruntled customer is demanding you call him back. What values do you check in with to make this decision?

Key Learning Points:

- Your values and beliefs were developed from the time you were a child; however, they can change over time.
- Your beliefs determine your thoughts, and your thoughts determine your actions. Your values and beliefs will influence your reactions, decisions, and the priorities you set as a leader.
- Defining your values gives you an opportunity to reflect on whether they are currently serving you. It is an exercise in awareness that enables you to change or focus on what is important to you now.
- Your top three core values will determine your life and career priorities.
- A personal signature statement is a tool that will help you integrate your core values into your leadership role.
- Consistent alignment with your values is the key to becoming an authentic leader.

Call for Courage

Staff Mob

Making tough decisions as a leader is nearly a daily occurrence. In tough times when budgets are tight, there is a lot at stake when making decisions about staff and their livelihoods. Around 2008, the country was in a devastating downturn, and the programs I was leading were hit hard with budget reductions. With each reduction, I was responsible for coming up with a budget that included a plan to match the budget. I had been a leader in the department for about 14 years when we were hit with yet another significant funding reduction. I gathered my administrative team, and we began to discuss the problem. I started by setting parameters for the solutions that we came up with: no staff out the door, no reduction of service to our children and families. With those 2 parameters in mind, our very creative team was able to come up with solutions that met both conditions.

The next step was to present the plan to my boss, who in turn had to inform the unions. After several conversations and more data collection, my boss gave me approval to present the information to staff. From past experience with this group, I knew the conversation was not going to be easy. Despite the fact that the plan included no one losing their job, it did include a few reductions in contracts. The presentation went as expected, and there were some very angry reactions. Staff accused me of not caring about anyone other than myself, protecting administration, and on and on. It's not easy delivering tough messages. I was able to gather my courage because I knew I was following my core values of truth, service, and relationships. It wasn't that I had to deliver the tough message, because that is just a part of being a leader. How I delivered the message, with respect and confidence, was the determinant of the impact on the organization as a whole. Courage helped me do just that.

Point of Courage: making hard decisions, standing behind the decision, listening to the feedback without defensiveness, and delivering the message with respect.

Chapter Two

AUTHENTICITY: CONSCIOUSNESS AND CREDIBILITY ARE KEY

"Authenticity is the single most important quality of leadership. You cannot 'get authentic' by delivering a great speech. It is demonstrated day-to-day through thousands of micro-behaviors."

– Bob Kidder

WHEN I THINK of authenticity, I think of something that is "an original." If I am looking at an authentic painting or artifact, I know it's from the original source, not a re-creation. To illustrate authenticity on a lighter note, if I'm hungry for the authentic cuisine of my roots, a Philadelphia cheesesteak or shoo-fly-pie, for example, nothing short of the original will satisfy my taste. In fact, whenever I see "Philadelphia cheesesteak" on a menu, my mouth starts to water and I get excited with anticipation of that first bite. More often than not, and to the chagrin of my dining partner, disappointment quickly ensues, and I feel the need to express my opinion about the inauthenticity of said "Philadelphia cheesesteak." If the server is not from the east coast, a quizzical look is all I usually get.

Reflecting on the consciously authentic people I've known in my life, the first person I think about is my Aunt Anita. She was my mother's sister, the youngest of three. As early as I can remember, Aunt Anita was an independent woman with a deep belief in God and a compassionate spirit. She lived with my grandma and was her primary caretaker. When we would visit my grandma in the small coal-mining town where they lived, Aunt Anita would always be there to greet us with a smile. Her personality was both exuberant and humble at the same time. I remember feeling that she was different, special, and unique. As I spent more time with her, my admiration grew. Most women at that time were married and "keeping house." That was the expected norm, but not so for Aunt Anita. She had her own path to follow. She captured me with her stories about taking her rowboat out fishing, being the only woman to go deer or bear hunting with the guys, and being on a bowling team. Any time I fell in "dis-favor" with my parents, she would send me a card signed, God's and my love always, Aunt Anita. I knew what to expect from my aunt—kindness, compassion, and an honesty that was ever consistent. My trust in her never wavered. She recently turned 75, went hunting this past season, and is still on a bowling team. In a recent call, she informed me with disappointment in her voice that her bowling average is now only 158. I don't think I've ever bowled a 158, let alone hit that as an average!

It's only when I've reflected on my own core values and leadership behaviors that I realize how much of Aunt Anita lives in me. As a leader, being honest, trustworthy, caring, and consistent run deep in my core. I learned to trust my inner core, develop my spiritual connection, and use those aspects to establish my authentic foundation to guide my behavior.

What is Conscious Authenticity?

The word "conscious" comes from the Latin root word *conscius*, meaning "knowing inwardly," and the word "authenticity" comes from the Greek root word *authentikos*, meaning "original, genuine."

The Merriam Webster dictionary defines conscious as:

"perceiving, apprehending, or noticing with a degree of controlled thought or observation." Synonyms: aware, mindful and defines authenticity as:

"true to one's own personality, spirit, or character." Synonyms: trustworthiness, truthfulness, genuine, real

I believe that conscious authenticity is being aware of and informed by your inner self and knowing that you are connected to a higher source. It is a deeper knowing, an awareness of a consciousness connected to something bigger than ourselves. In that deeper place, we find ethics that are meant to guide us toward principles that promote the highest good for all.

Psychologists Brian Goldman and Michael Kernis describe authenticity that is connected to action:

"Authenticity is the unimpeded operation of one's true or core self and one's daily enterprise."

Dr. Martin Luther King, Jr. talks about the application of conscience to decision making:

"There comes a time when one must take a position that is neither safe, nor politic, nor popular, but he must take it because conscience tells him it is right."

When talking about a person who is authentic, I think of someone who "walks his or her talk." A consciously authentic person is one who grounds their core values in an ethos of spirit for the benefit of the greater good and models those values in their behavior.

Characteristics of a consciously authentic person:

- genuine
- honest
- trustworthy
- humble
- proud of their uniqueness
- willing to be vulnerable
- guided to action by their inner self, rather than external triggers
- comfortable expressing their own opinion respectfully

Thinking globally, the authentic people who first come to mind are Mother Teresa, Martin Luther King, Jr., Gandhi, and Princess Diana. From their actions, we can discern that they believed in service, justice, and compassion. Their actions matched their espoused values.

Why Conscious Authenticity is Important for Leaders

"Credibility is currency for leadership."

– John Maxwell

A primary goal of a leader is to influence others to action. While an inauthentic leader can appear authentic and gain a followership, the results can be devastating. Take the most heinous example of Hitler. Even though he had people who followed him with his illusion of authenticity, he was so far removed from his conscious self, thus resulting in devastation and the deaths of millions. He was an evil dictator who preyed on people's fears. The deep scars imbedded as a result of lack of conscience in the hands of power have remained a part of the roots of racial and ethnic bias today.

As a consciously authentic leader, you will have influence in carrying out your organization's mission. You will gain significant credibility as you develop trust with people, which is the heartbeat of being authentic. People are not only willing, but also eager to follow guidance and direction from a consciously authentic leader.

As a leader, being authentic establishes your inner compass when faced with challenging decisions. Your inner core will guide you, and your actions will model those deep beliefs and values. For example:

- Honesty as a core value: if you are faced with a problem involving a mistake, you will more easily own up to it without a need to place blame on someone else. Your actions are guided by your core value, which means that you take responsibility.
- Truth as a core value: if you have an opinion that is different than one someone is stating, you are comfortable to share your own view. If your core value of truth is paired with another value of respect, for example, you will share your opinion in a respectful way. An authentic leader who values truth can be counted on to follow through on whatever they say they will do. Authenticity is "walking your talk," so following through is the congruent action of truth as a value.

Characteristics of an Authentic Leader	Authentic Behavior	Inauthentic Behavior
Honesty	Admits to mistakes	Blames mistakes on others
Willing to express their opinion	Respectfully shares their point of view	Remains silent in fear of criticism
Willing to be vulnerable	Open to criticism	Defensive when hearing criticism
Trustworthy	Follows through on what they say they will do	Inconsistent - cannot be counted on to do what they say they will
Makes decisions from inner guidance	Bases the decision on a grounded core value	Makes decisions based on what they think other people want

Authentic leaders are open and transparent – if you are initiating a change, you will be open about what is going on and why. You will be open to criticism and feedback, which will give you a better product and a more inclusive organization. In fact, it is of critical importance for leaders to create a safe space for people to freely share their comments and concerns. A parent in a program I led was disgruntled about something. When I asked her why she didn't share her concerns earlier, she said, "You have to nurture people to tell you the truth." That interaction was a significant point of learning for me. The wisdom in that comment underscored my responsibility as a leader to connect with my core value of truth and make sure my open-door policy was a safe space for anyone to share his or her honest feedback.

Being authentic doesn't mean you will always have a smile on your face. Leaders are human; and there will be times that you are frustrated, angry, or sad. An authentic leader expresses a range of emotions. It is the pairing of being authentic and conscious that is important. Being robotic, without displaying any emotions, garners mistrust, as people will second-guess your authenticity.

There were times as a leader when my emotions took over and I needed to learn how to express them in a way that allowed my authenticity to show, without adversely impacting my staff. I recall one situation when I was particularly frustrated with a directive I was given from my boss. I was told to make changes that I didn't agree with, and I became visibly frustrated and expressed my anger in front of my leadership team. In the faces of the people near me I could see feelings of discomfort. I quickly apologized; however, one of them said, "It's okay, Tracy; this is a really hard situation." The trust she had in me allowed me to be authentic, even if it meant openly sharing frustration.

There were other hard times I went through with my staff where the vulnerability of being authentic challenged me. When a staff member lost her husband to a heart attack without warning and several others lost their battles to cancer, I had to face balancing being the "I have it all together, person in charge" with the devastating feelings for the people I cared so much about. I remember visiting one woman in the hospital who was nearing the end of her battle with cancer. My stomach churned as I fought back the tears that wanted to fall down my face. We sat together; I held her hand and let a few tears fall. We both knew there were no words to be shared, only the authentic feeling of deep sadness.

It was common to hear people say that they could count on me to be "real." They said they didn't have to guess if I had some hidden agenda. I attribute those comments to the fact that I led with an open heart. I was authentic.

Behavior that is congruent with your core values and beliefs is essential in order to be an authentic and effective leader. When values and actions are incongruent, the words of Ralph Waldo Emerson ring true,

"Your actions speak so loudly I can't hear what you are saying."

As a leader, when your words don't match your actions, doubt and mistrust become the norm. Conversely, a leader who is consciously authentic and displays congruency between principled words and integrity in action creates an environment of loyalty and trust.

Reflection Activity #1

Recognizing Authenticity

Name three people who you believe are **authentic**.

_____

_____

_____

List the specific **authentic** behaviors you observe in each person you listed above.

_____

_____

_____

Name three people who you believe exhibit **inauthentic** behaviors.

_____

_____

_____

List the specific **inauthentic** behaviors you observe in each person you listed above.

_____

_____

_____

Reflection Activity #2

Recognizing Authenticity

List your own behaviors that are **authentic**.

_____

_____

_____

List your own behaviors that are **inauthentic**.

_____

_____

_____

What changes will you make to eliminate or transform your inauthentic behaviors?

_____

_____

_____

Questions to Reflect on Your Authenticity:

Courage: Do you speak up even when you're facing fear of ridicule?
If not, why?

Transparency: Do you reveal your thoughts, feelings, and expectations?
If not, why?

Feedback: Do you welcome constructive feedback?
If not, why?

Self-Correction: Do you feel comfortable revisiting something you've previously said?
If not, why?

Assertion: Do you easily state what you want and what you don't want?

Linking Authenticity to Credibility

My top three core values are:

    1.   _____

    2.   _____

    3.   _____

My Top Three Values in Action

Core Value	What the Core Value Means to Me	Behaviors that Demonstrate the Core Value

Reflection Activity #3

Values and Behaviors Alignment

Set a time at the end of each day for reflection. Rate yourself on a scale of 0-5 for how well you lived each of your top three values that day.
(0 not very well - 5 very well)

Core Value	M	T	W	T	F	S	S

Introspection and awareness are the first steps to developing behaviors that reflect your values. Reflecting on your day/week, what, if anything, would you change to better align your behaviors with your values to increase authenticity and credibility?

Key Learning Points

- To be consciously authentic, you must know your values and live by them.
- Authenticity creates trust. Those you lead will know what is important to you and what to expect when working with you.
- Authenticity requires openness—stating what you are doing and why, as well as openly accepting and welcoming feedback and criticism.
- A lack of authenticity results in inconsistent behavior and decisions, which result in a lack of respect, trust, and loyalty.
- An authentic leader is one who is:
  - Honest
  - States their opinion
  - Admits their mistakes
  - Trustworthy
  - Consistent
  - Open to criticism
  - Uses values as a guide when making decisions

To increase your authenticity:
- Accept yourself and live congruently with who you are and are not.
- Be proud of your strengths and make a commitment to change those aspects you are not proud of.
- Be aware of what is holding you back.
- Don't let the world turn you into something you are not—make sure your actions represent who you are, not what someone wants you to be.
- Discover your values and consistently act according to them.

Call for Courage

My First Act of Courage

When I was five years old, I used to walk a few blocks to the neighborhood corner store to get an ice cream bar. Every time I went into that store, The Market Basket, I heard the familiar voice of John, the owner, call out my nickname, "Hey Tomato." One day I had selected my ice cream and when I went to pay for it, John told me the price had gone up by five cents. I was aghast; a nickel was a lot of money to a five year old back then. John explained that the ice cream company had raised the price and there was nothing he could do about it. I was really bothered by it, so when he told me I could write a letter to the company, Dolly Madison, I decided to do just that. The company responded with a letter explaining that the cost of sugar and milk had gone up, which is why they had to raise their prices. Even though it felt a little scary to write that letter, by finding the courage to do it, I at least felt satisfied that I did something about a situation that I felt was wrong.

Point of Courage: Doing something new, out of my comfort zone—having support from a trusted source helped me find my courage to use my authentic voice.

Chapter Three

COMMUNICATION

"A leader doesn't just get the message across—a leader is the message."

– Warren Bennis

WHEN I LOOK back on the early days of my leadership journey, I shake my head and laugh—a nervous laugh, that is. I picture myself as a whirlwind, a tornado, moving so quickly that I was a blur that zipped past anyone in my path. Imagine someone who is barely 5'2" tall and weighing 100 pounds, talking and moving at the speed of light. Yes, that was me.

"Tracy, slow down" was something I heard often. I also heard questions like, "Are you angry? What's wrong?" I never understood those questions. Inside, I was fine; I was just getting the job done. I wasn't angry. I was feeling calm and focused, but my body language and tone conveyed something completely different. This was one hard lesson for me to learn. I talked and moved so fast that when I tried to *slow* down, it felt like I was in s-l-o-w motion. Everyone assured me that what I thought was slow motion was actually talking and moving at a normal pace, but my head and body took a long time to connect to that concept. There was such disconnect between what I was trying to communicate and how people interpreted my message. If I was going to be the leader I knew I was inside, I needed to learn new communication skills, and fast!

I can now thankfully say that "was" me because I was most fortunate to have had mentors, teachers, and friends who held up the mirror for me and were patient as I learned new skills and found more effective ways to communicate. It was not the fast process I had hoped for, but I did learn those new communication skills and have anchored them as my "new normal."

As a leadership coach, communication is the most often requested training and coaching need from my clients. I frequently hear:

"I can't get my staff to listen to me."
"I have an employee who is so difficult, and I just don't know what to do."
"I don't like confrontation."
"Can you help me fix these people?"

Do those questions and comments sound familiar? As leaders, effective communication is essential in producing quality results in your organization. In fact, educator and author Stephen Covey asserts, *"Communication is the most important skill in life."*

In this chapter, I will walk you through the maze that makes up communication, its complexity, and the importance of understanding your communication style and the style of those you lead. You'll learn the importance of listening and strategies to deal with conflict. When you apply these skills, your communication will be received as you intend it to be.

What is Effective Communication?

Communication is an effective exchange of information. I define effective and conscious communication as:

"...a mutually respectful transfer of information where all parties have the same understanding of the information."

As easy as that sounds, all too often our "effective communication" gets derailed and leads us down a path of misunderstanding or conflict.

Alan Greenspan sums up the complexity of communication this way:

"I know you think you understand what you thought I said, but I'm not sure you realize that what you heard is not what I meant."

Greenspan's quote illustrates that often we communicate with someone and think we are on the same page and in agreement, only to find out later that's not the case.

I remember times when I've talked with an employee, given them directions for a task, and when the project was delivered, it wasn't what I had asked for. I had apparently forgotten the part of my definition of communication that states, *"…where all parties have the same understanding of the information."* I assumed that because I said it, the other person knew what I meant.

As a leader, you might relate to the following conversation:

Manager sends an email to an employee: "I need the audit report ASAP."

The day passes, and the manager hasn't received the report and is now getting more and more frustrated and calls the employee in to the office.

Manager: Where is that report? I said I wanted it ASAP.

Employee: I am doing it as soon as I can; I have other priorities.

Manager: Don't you realize ASAP means immediately?

Employee: Why didn't you say that?

Effective communication is at the core of the results we get, at work and at home. A participant in a recent training I was leading observed, "This isn't just for work; these are life skills you're teaching us. We can use them anywhere."

The Sender and Receiver:

Communication is complex and has multiple layers that influence what is said and what is heard. The basics—there are two or more people involved in a communication, a sender and a receiver. The sender and the receiver each have competing elements going on at the same time that influence their communication. Many of these issues are invisible, subconscious. The unseen elements are known as "root issues." Combine the impact of our root issues, differences in communication style, tone, and body language and you have a clear recipe for miscommunication.

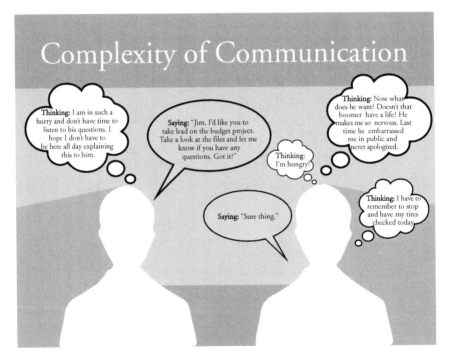

A communication exchange between people includes both verbal and non-verbal cues. Verbal cues include words and tonality. Non-verbal cues are conveyed by body language.

From his studies in the 1970's, Dr. Albert Mehrabian quantified the impact of verbal and non-verbal cues on communication to the following degree:

Words 7%	Tone 38%	Body Language 55%

Words make up only 7% of the understanding of a communication. That low percentage tells us that words have some importance; however, *how* we say something is much more important than *what* we say. In addition, the words we use are diminished and become meaningless without authenticity. Tone and body language are the cues that convey the level of authenticity.

As a manager, a common practice I had when I walked into my office every morning was to check in with people and say hello and ask how they were. I genuinely cared about them and would take time to hear their response. The fact that I made eye contact and had a relaxed posture showed them that my words, "How are you?" were authentic. On the contrary, had I asked that same question while walking past them, the sincerity of my intent would justifiably be called into question.

Ninety-three percent of how communication is understood is deciphered from tone and body language. For example, if someone is talking to you and looking at their watch or glancing around the room, their body language might be construed that you are not important to them. Incongruence in body language, tone, and the words we use lead to miscommunication.

Two examples of incongruent communication cues:

Words	Body Language	Meaning
I respect your opinion	Rolling your eyes	Inauthentic – your words and body language don't match

Words said with Tone	Meaning
I AM listening	The tone used in accentuating I "AM" conveys defensiveness and shuts down communication.

Communication Starters for Tone and Body Language Issues
Cues:

When we are in the heat of a discussion with emotions present, it is difficult to know what to say in the moment. The following examples can be used as communication starters in challenging situations.

- Button pushing words or statements

Statement: "You just don't care."
Pause before responding…
Response: "Actually, I do care. Help me understand why you think I don't."

- Inflection issue

Statement: "I AM listening!"
Pause before responding…
Response: "I appreciate that you want to listen. Was there something I said that frustrated you?"

- Body language

Situation: Someone is crossing their arms and looking annoyed.
Pause before responding

Response: "I notice you're crossing your arms; are you cold or is it something else?"

- Making your own cues transparent

Situation: To make sure any unintended body language you may have won't be misinterpreted.

Response: "I have a lot of things going on today, so if I seem distracted, I wanted you to be aware of that. I'll do my best to stay focused."

Root Issues

Understanding the root issues related to a communication is critical to the success of that communication.

Root issues are the underlying or hidden conditions and elements that influence what is said and what is heard.

Root issues can include influences from our beliefs, values, culture, gender, generation, unresolved issues from the past, or what happened before leaving for work that day. A power or status differential can also impact the communication. As an example, if someone has had negative experiences with an authority figure in their past, something you say may trigger them. If they are unaware of that trigger, they may be responding to you as if you were the person whom they had a negative experience with.

I experienced this situation with a woman I supervised years ago. I asked her about a task she was supposed to have completed by a certain date. She became visibly upset. She cried and starting saying things like, "Nothing I ever do is good enough. I should just quit because I'm sure you think I'll fail anyway."

I was quite taken aback because this was a person who I valued and who usually did get her assignments done on time. Her dramatic reaction left me speechless. It wasn't until a few days later that she asked if she could meet with me. She apologized for her over-reaction and told me that her parents always criticized her. They were never happy with her decisions and told her that she would never amount to anything. Needless to say, I was humbled by the honesty and vulnerability she shared with me. I also learned a lesson about how powerful root issues can be and how they can show up completely unexpected.

The interaction I shared demonstrates how root issues can block communication and lead to misunderstandings or conflict. Root issues can be especially problematic if a person is unaware of them. Those hidden issues can bubble up when triggered by something someone says or does unknowingly. Root issues are like an onion; as you go deeper into an issue, it's like peeling layer after layer.

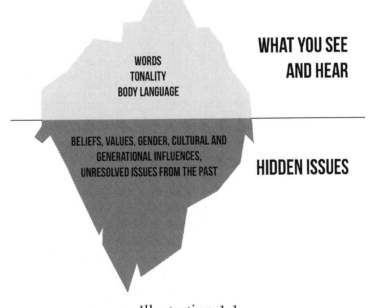

WORDS
TONALITY
BODY LANGUAGE

WHAT YOU SEE AND HEAR

BELIEFS, VALUES, GENDER, CULTURAL AND
GENERATIONAL INFLUENCES,
UNRESOLVED ISSUES FROM THE PAST

HIDDEN ISSUES

Illustration 1.1

Illustration 1.1 uses an iceberg to show the seen and unseen (root issues) of a communication. We can see and hear words, tonality, and body language. What we can't see are a person's values, beliefs, unresolved issues, and other influences.

How Can We Become Aware of Our Root Issues?

To become aware of your root issues, it is necessary to be mindful of how your culture, values, and beliefs influence you. By reflecting on your life and significant memories that may have impacted you, you get in touch with deeper parts of yourself. Developing self-awareness enables you to look at a situation from a different perspective. Looking at your deeper self takes courage. Once exposed, hidden beliefs and biases can be transformed to help you change your behavior and how it impacts your communication.

Examples that may negatively impact communication:

Root issue: You have been taught not to question authority.

Potential impact on communication: If someone you supervise questions you, you might take that as challenging and inappropriate, rather than the fact that they are simply seeking to understand something.

Root issue: You had a negative interaction with someone and didn't resolve it.

Potential impact on communication: You're hanging on to negative feelings toward that person so no matter what they say, you might over-react.

Root issue: You grew up in a culture where being loud and boisterous was a regular way of communicating.

Potential impact on communication: You may be perceived as being an angry person.

Reflect on your own values, unresolved issues, and culture. How do they impact your communication?

Using your awareness of your root issues that impact communication, what will you change or do differently to minimize any negative impact they have?

FOUR COMMUNICATION STYLES

Each of us has a primary style we use during communication. There is no "best" style. Each style is unique and offers strengths and challenges. We also have characteristics of other styles, a combination of styles. It is important to know your primary style so you can accentuate the strengths of that style and minimize the challenges to communicate more effectively.

The informal assessment presented will help you determine your primary and secondary communication styles. It is meant to help you identify the style you communicate with most often. Think about your work setting when responding to the assessment statements.

Assessing Your Communication Style

This informal assessment is meant to help you identify the style you communicate with most often at work. Check the statement in each pair that is <u>most typical</u> of your communication style. There are no right or wrong answers.

1. _____ I find solutions to problems quickly.
2. _____ I am indecisive and take my time when making decisions.

3. _____ I enjoy developing relationships and working on a team.
4. _____ I prefer to work on my own.

5. _____ I prefer to lead or facilitate a meeting.
6. _____ I prefer to be a participant in a meeting so I can share all of my good ideas.

7. _____ I prefer that people get right to the point when they talk to me.
8. _____ I prefer that people share all of the facts and details when they talk to me.

9. _____ People tell me I am a good listener.
10. _____ People call me a chatterbox.

11. _____ I am decisive and take action quickly based on the current information.
12. _____ I tend to be impulsive when making decisions, especially if the idea results in a fun project.

13. _____ I am comfortable when people express their emotions around me.
14. _____ I tend not to express my emotions openly and prefer to stick to logic.

15. _____ I process problems in a methodical way before responding.
16. _____ I tend to respond spontaneously when faced with a problem.

17. ____ Listening to people and their feelings in a conversation is most important.

18. ____ If the conversation gets too serious, I will lighten it up because I want to have fun.

19. ____ I most enjoy working with people who focus on the task.

20. ____ I most enjoy working with people who want to have fun.

21. ____ I am highly expressive when I communicate.

22. ____ I am reserved in conversation.

23. ____ I network with others to find the best solution.

24. ____ I network with others to have fun.

25. ____ In my workspace, you will see pictures of my family, pets, and personal artifacts.

26. ____ In my workspace, you will see pencils, calculators, and planning tools.

27. ____ I like to multitask, handling several projects at the same time.

28. ____ I like to focus on one issue at a time.

29. ____ If I hear a good idea, I will put it into action immediately.

30. ____ All new ideas have to be tested before implemented.

31. ____ I make decisions quickly but can change if new, logical facts emerge.

32. ____ It is important to me to hear everyone's opinion before making a decision.

33. _____ I like to hear the details.

34. _____ I prefer abstract—the more theoretical, the better.

35. _____ I am responsive to others' interests and concerns.

36. _____ I am more focused on my interests and concerns.

Scoring Your Communication Style Assessment

To find your style of communication, mark the item number that you circled for each pair in the assessment. Enter the total **number of items** you circled in each style below and then enter that total in the column labeled "total." The highest number you can have in any style is 9.

<u>Style</u>	<u>Circle Your Answer below</u>	<u>Total</u>
Style #1 (Driver)	1 – 5 – 7 – 11 – 19 – 27 – 29 – 31 – 36	_____
Style #2 (Analyzer)	4 – 8 – 14 – 15 – 22 – 26 – 28 - 30 – 33	_____
Style #3 (Harmonizer)	2 – 3 – 9 – 13 – 17 – 23 – 25 – 32 – 35	_____
Style #4 (Energizer)	6 – 10 – 12 – 16 – 18 – 20 – 21 – 24 – 34	_____

The style with the highest number of points represents your primary style of communication. The style with the second highest number of points indicates your secondary style of communication. There is no "best" style of communication.

Each style has its strengths and challenges. The good news is that we can use our primary style and benefit from its strengths, while developing the skills of other styles that will help us minimize the challenges of our primary style.

My primary style is _____

My secondary style is _____

CHARACTERISTICS OF COMMUNICATION STYLES

Common characteristics of a person with a Driver communication style:

- directive
- results oriented
- decisive risk taker
- values getting the job done
- enjoys being in charge

Common characteristics of a person with an Analyzer communication style:

- methodical, planner
- values accuracy
- cautious
- needs details
- logical

Common characteristics of a person with a Harmonizer communication style:

- relationship oriented
- good listener
- enjoys a strong network of people
- cares about how people feel
- sensitive

Common characteristics of a person with an Energizer communication style:

- high energy
- values the fun in a project
- creative—all about the possibilities
- loves to celebrate
- expressive

Strategies to Minimize the Challenges of Your Style

The following strategies can be used to minimize the challenges of each communication style.

If you are a Driver:
- slow down the pace of your speaking and moving
- develop patience and sensitivity
- develop your ability to listen

If you are an Analyzer:
- apply policies as guidelines whenever possible, not hard and fast rules
- develop empathy
- done is better than perfect

If you are a Harmonizer:
- be aware of being overly sensitive
- increase your acceptance of change
- know that shifting people to focus on the task does not discount your relationship with them

If you are an Energizer:
- stay focused on one idea
- do more verifying
- follow through on tasks

Strategies to Increase Success When Communicating With Each Style

Use the following strategies to increase your likelihood of success when communicating with someone who has a style that is different from yours.

When communicating with a Driver:
- start your conversation with the bottom line
- keep the conversation brief
- express your needs directly

When communicating with an Analyzer:
- be precise and have your facts ready, no surprises
- use logic when presenting the situation
- be patient, don't rush them to a decision

When communicating with a Harmonizer:
- begin your conversation with talk that builds rapport
- emphasize the relationship angle of your idea
- be open and cooperative to their ideas

When communicating with an Energizer:
- allow them time to fully express their idea
- validate their creativity
- let them know there will be a time to discuss celebrations

Conversation Starters for Each Communication Style

Helping people attend to your style:
If you are a Driver, you can say:
- "I'd like to hear more about those details you are sharing in a minute. Would you please share what it is you want first and then we'll get to the details?"

If you are an Analyzer, you can say:
- "Please give me an overview of the project so I can listen with that in mind."

If you are a Harmonizer, you can say:
- "I can see that you are very stressed about this project. Is there anything I can do to help you?"

If you are an Energizer, you can say:
- "I have so many ideas about this project, when will I have an opportunity to share them?"

To communicate more effectively with other styles, begin with a statement that will help them listen more attentively.
Communicating with a Driver:
- "I'd like to share three brief but important points before I get to the bottom line."

Communicating with an Analyzer:
- "I realize you want to get all of the details finished; however, I need the project completed in an hour."

Communicating with a Harmonizer:
- "I am so excited about this project and how it will give all of us an opportunity to work together more often."

Communicating with an Energizer:
- "I know you have a lot of really good ideas on this subject, so I allocated time on the agenda to hear them."

Recognizing and Working With Other Communication Styles

Think about someone you work with who has a style that you find challenging. What specifically about that person's communication style challenges you?

What strategies can you use to communicate more positively with this person?

Think about a friend or family member who has a style that you find challenging. What specifically about that person's communication style challenges you?

What strategies can you use to communicate more positively with this person?

LISTENING

Listening is a skill that enables you to be changed by what other people say. Listening requires openness, a non-judgmental state, and both inner and outer quiet. The statement, "we are born with two ears and one mouth for a reason" underscores the point.

What do you notice about these two words?
LISTEN   SILENT

Each word is made up of the same letters. The connection between listening and the importance of being quiet is paramount.

When we talk to someone, we have an intention, something we want to convey. It might be to inform, convince, or to educate. The same is true with listening. Whether we are aware of it or not, we listen with a specific intent. Three of the most utilized listening intents include listening to *win*, to *persuade*, and to *learn*.

Your listening intent is your filter; it is one way you assign meaning to what you hear. Whatever filter you are listening from, it will play a direct role in the result you get in any communication.

Elements of Listening Intents

Listening to win:

When your intent is to win, you are in a fight or flight mode. You argue and debate, use a questioning strategy to probe for weakness. You want to win at any cost, even if it negatively impacts the relationship with whomever you are communicating.

Example:
A manager is talking to an employee about being 15 minutes late to work every day. The employee is listening "to win."

Manager: You have been coming in 15 minutes late for the past week, and I need you to be on time.

Employee: That's not true; I was here at 8:00 today.

Manager: There have been several days you've been late. Everyone else is here on time. I expect you to be, too.

Employee: The staff over on the other side of the building are allowed to come in late.

Manager: Our company policy says everyone needs to arrive at 8:00.

Employee: Not everyone is following the policy.

In this situation, no matter what the manager says, the employee argues and listens for the weakness to win his point.

Listening to persuade:

When your intent is to persuade, you are in a reactionary mode. You discuss to convince or win over. Your questioning strategy is to probe for an opportunity for closure. You will try to negotiate a compromise.

Example:
A manager wants to persuade an employee to take on a project.

Manager: I'd like you to take on the auditing project for the review that is coming up.

Employee: I'm already on several projects, and frankly I'm tired of being on a team and counting on other people to get the work done.

Manager: Well, actually this is a great project for you then. You can do it independently, and I'll even take you off of one of the other teams if you'd like.

Employee: Okay, I like working independently, and I appreciate you taking me off another team project.

The manager listened to what was important to the employee. When the employee mentioned that he didn't like working on a team, the boss emphasized that the project she wanted him to do could be done independently and also made the case by saying she would remove the employee from one other team project. This enabled her to persuade him to take on the project more easily.

Listening to learn:
When your intent is to learn, you are in an awareness mode. You discuss to understand and use a questioning strategy to clarify or gain insight.

Example:
A manager is talking with a customer who is complaining about the terrible service they received.

Manager: How may I help you?

Customer: I had the worst service ever yesterday. I've been coming here for many years, and I have never been treated so rudely. You used to have great customer service, but now it is just awful.

Manager: I'm sorry to hear you had such an experience. No one likes to be treated rudely. Please help me understand more about what specifically happened.

Customer: I stood in line for 15 minutes; and when I finally got to the register, your clerk answered the phone to help someone else and ignored me.

Manager: You sound very frustrated, and I can certainly understand that. Waiting in a long line is hard and then not being acknowledged made it even worse. I appreciate you bringing this issue to my attention, and I will make sure to follow up.

Customer: Thank you.

The manager asked questions to fully understand the specifics of the complaint. When she got clarification, she used it to acknowledge and validate the customer's frustration.

As a leader, maintaining positive relationships are key. Being fully aware of your listening intent will help you use strategies that achieve the results you want, while at the same time maintaining or building positive relationships. Finally, the best advice regarding listening comes from Thoreau:

"Never say anything unless it will improve on silence."

DEALING WITH DIFFICULT PEOPLE/CONFLICT

Dealing with "difficult people" is the number one problem I hear from my clients. When someone tells me they don't know how to deal with that "one" problem person, I always begin with, "Tell me more about what makes them so difficult." The responses are similar, and difficult people are labeled as argumentative, uncooperative, rude, gossipy, or they don't listen or do what they are asked to do. After acknowledging the frustration my clients are feeling, I ask them, "Do you think you have ever been a 'difficult person'?"

At some point, most of us have probably been that "difficult person" in a conversation. It is an important point to make because we think of these challenging individuals as "them," "those people," someone other than ourselves. When we understand the importance of separating out the problematic behavior from the person, we can begin to find strategies to communicate. *A person is more than the challenge they are presenting, and it is the problem behavior we need to focus on to get results.*

The other factor that is important is our beliefs about conflict and the impact it can have in communication. For example, if I believe conflict is negative and unproductive, that is how I will approach the conversation. My emotional state will prepare me for battle, and my behavior will reflect body language that is closed and shut down. The results will likely be non-productive. Conversely, if I believe that conflict is no more than a difference in opinion, I will be more open to the discussion.

Strategies for Responding to Difficult Situations

The most important skill to effectively deal with conflict is to learn to *respond*, rather than *react*. When we think about what we want to say while the other person is talking, and they are doing the same, the conversation is like a tennis match; each side reacts to what was served in their direction. *Responding* is more thoughtful, and the listening intent is focused on seeking 'to understand'.

The following strategies are useful tools to defuse or respond to conflict.

- Reframing - allows you to separate emotion and shift unproductive beliefs into empowering beliefs:
    - Reframe your belief about how you define conflict – from thinking that conflict is negative and unproductive, to thinking that conflict can be an opportunity to look at things in another way or to solve a problem.
    - If you believe you are a victim and the other person is the enemy, reframe your thinking to believe that rather than being an enemy who is out to get you, the other person is simply bringing the issue forward.

- Compassionate listening – If the person is sharing heavy feelings or burdens, you might say, "That sounds like it was hard to deal with." It shows them that you care about what they are saying.

- Clarifying – If you're not sure of some of the details of what is being said, you might say, "Help me understand more about…" This conveys to the person that you really want to know what they are saying.

- Acknowledging – If you want to be neutral but accepting of whatever the person is saying, you might say, "I can see that was a frustrating situation." In this statement, you recognize the emotion associated with a given situation and the person knows you are hearing them accurately.

- Validate or normalize – If the person is sharing strong feelings and you can authentically relate, you might say, "I think I might feel the same way if that happened to me." Validation helps the person feel supported.

The strategy you use will depend on the conversation and the need of the person you are talking to. Whatever strategy you use to respond to the conflict or difficult conversation, you want to make sure you resolve, rather than just settle, the issue. If you simply settle, it will likely become a root issue that will present itself in the future. Confirm with the person that they feel the situation has been resolved. If it is not, continue until it is or agree to revisit the issue in the future.

Conversation Starters in Confrontational Situations

The following strategies can be used to respond to a difficult situation:
- Tell me more…
- Help me understand…
- I can see/hear you feel (angry, frustrated).
- I think I might feel like that if it happened to me.
- I appreciate you bringing that issue forward.

Responding to someone who is speaking disrespectfully to you
- "I want to hear what you have to say; however, what you just said sounded demeaning to me. Can you please say it again in a different way?"

Needing to tell someone information that will be hard for them to hear
- "I want you to know that I value your efforts on this project. I do have one piece of it that I'd like to

review with you." (Say what the issue is and let them respond.)

Taking responsibility for your actions

- "I want to apologize; what I just said came out all wrong. I'd like to say it again in another way."

Giving and Receiving Feedback

When feedback is given with sincerity and positive intent, it is an opportunity for growth. It can affirm that what we are doing is effective or help us see the gap between the results we think we are getting and the results we are actually getting. Equally important is how we *give* feedback, as well as how we *respond* to feedback.

In giving feedback, **timing** is everything, followed by the setting in which it is given. There needs to be readiness in the person to whom you are giving feedback. If they are running out the door to take care of a sick relative or get to an appointment, the timing may not be the most productive to give feedback. In regard to the setting, it is usually best to be given in a private place.

> During a coaching session, a client shared with me that every time her supervisor has something to tell her, he would call her into his office at 4:25. Her shift ended at 4:30, and it infuriated her that she was being kept late, not to mention that it was usually something negative being shared, and she ended up going home grouchy and frustrated.

The purpose of giving feedback is to deliver a message and have it received as intended. When the feedback is the delivery of difficult or negative news, it is especially important to help the receiver be at ease.

Consider these two scenarios for giving feedback:

> A supervisor needs to talk to an employee about inaccurate information in a report the employee recently completed.

Situation 1.

The supervisor sends an email asking the employee (whose communication style is Analyzer) to come to his office ASAP.

The employee enters the office. The supervisor is behind his desk, working on his computer. He looks up and tells the employee to sit down. He throws the report across his desk and says, "This report is full of errors. I've never seen such unprofessional work from you. You need to fix every error and get it back to me by tomorrow noon."

How do you think this employee is feeling?

Situation 2 – same scenario with a different approach:

The supervisor calls the employee and asks them to come to his office before the end of the day to go over the report that was just submitted.

The employee walks into the office. The supervisor looks up, invites the employee to sit down, and turns his chair to face the employee.

Supervisor: "Thank you for coming in. I know you pride yourself on producing quality work, and I really appreciate that about you. I want to talk to you about the report you recently turned in. Was that a particularly difficult project?"

Employee: "Actually, yes, it was, plus I was working on too many things at once."

Supervisor: "I thought something was wrong. I found several errors, and I've marked them for you to correct. Do you want to review them with me now or look at them yourself?"

Employee: "I'll look at them and ask you if I need clarification."

Supervisor: "Okay, I need the corrections back by tomorrow noon. Do you need any support to get this done?"

Employee: "No, I'll make the corrections right away."

Supervisor: "Thank you, I appreciate your responsiveness."

How do you think the employee is feeling?

What are the differences in how the supervisor handled the situation?

Guidelines for Giving/Receiving Feedback

Giving Feedback
- Place and time – think about whether your office, their office, or a neutral location is best, pay attention to the best time of the meeting
- What is the communication style of the person receiving the feedback?
  - Driver: get right to the point
  - Analyzer: have data and specific details available
  - Harmonizer: focus on positive relationship
  - Energizer: since feedback can be about serious issues, it is important to know the secondary style of this person.
- Create readiness - start with rapport building, establish that you will be giving feedback and they will have time to respond
- Share a positive comment
  - "You've really stepped up to take on this project."
  - "I noticed your team is working hard on …
  - I appreciate having the opportunity to talk with you."

- Give constructive feedback
  - be specific
  - let them know this is your point of view
  - focus on the behavior, rather than the person
  - be respectful

- End the conversation with a positive comment – clarify the agreement and acknowledge/appreciate their cooperation with the agreement

Receiving Feedback
- Know how you receive feedback most openly, and let people who are giving you feedback know the best way to approach you
- Avoid being defensive or justifying
- Ask clarifying questions
- Summarize what you heard
- Assume positive intent, and thank the person for sharing their feedback
- Remember that this is about your *behavior,* not you

Responding to Challenges for Giving or Receiving Feedback

Even with positive intent, if the person giving feedback lacks the skill to do it, there will be problems with the communication.

The following strategies will help you respond, rather than react.

Issues from the person giving the feedback:

They start by telling you everything you did wrong. You are feeling defensive.

- Listen and ask clarifying questions
- Don't say anything until you can detach from the emotion. This is about them, not you.

They are not respectful in their delivery. You need to set a boundary.

- Ask them to stop, let them know you want to hear them; however, it's not okay for them to degrade you by saying what they are saying.

  "I respect that you are my (boss or colleague); however, it's important to me that I be spoken to with respect. I'm feeling disrespected when you say I'm (stupid/lazy/don't care)."

- Remind them that you wouldn't talk to them or anyone else with those words or that tone and you would appreciate it if they would start the conversation over in a respectful way.

Issues from the person receiving the feedback:

Not everyone is going to be eager to hear your feedback, no matter how positive your intent is. The following strategies can be used to respond in a way that can help them be more open to hearing what you have to say.

- They are shut down, with arms crossed and eyes looking down. You need to help them feel safe or they won't be able to hear you.
  - "Let me say again that I value your work and we all need reminders now and then. You are not (in trouble/going to lose your job).

"From your crossed arms and furrowed brow, it looks like you're not wanting to hear what I have to say. I really need you to hear me, and I'll give you an opportunity to respond."

They disagree with every observation you share.

- "I can hear that our perceptions of your behavior are different. You think your heavy sighing is because you are tired. It can also be perceived as a negative judgment on what was just said. If you are, indeed, that tired, and now know how it can be perceived, what can you do to minimize the chance you'll be misinterpreted?"

Giving Feedback – Practice Scenarios

Reflect on the scenarios below to practice using the communication strategies and the giving/receiving feedback guidelines you learned in this chapter. With the intent to be most effective, reflect on how you would respond.

1. A person you supervise has been coming late to meetings, and other staff members are complaining to you about it. The communication style of this person is Analyzer.

    What are the key points you would make when having a conversation with this person?

2. You have received sub-standard work from a person you supervise. The communication style of this person is Driver.

   What are the key points you would make when having a conversation with this person?

3. You have not been included in a recent decision that impacts you. You are upset and want to let your supervisor know how you feel. Your supervisor's communication style is Harmonizer.

   What are the key points you would make when having a conversation with this person?

4. You are working on a project with a few colleagues, and one of them is not meeting their timelines for the project. Your colleague's communication style is Energizer.

   What are the key points you would make when having a conversation with this person?

Key Learning Points:

- Effective communication is a mutually respectful transfer of information that results in all parties having the same understanding of what was communicated.
- Authentic communication includes tone, body language, and the words we use. All three must be congruent.
- Everyone has root issues that will influence what they say and how they interpret what was said.
- Understanding your communication style and the communication style of the person you're speaking to will help leaders effectively communicate with others.
- Your intention of listening will determine how you interpret the meaning of what was said.
- When dealing with difficult people or conflict, your approach will determine your outcome.
- It is possible to repair communication breakdowns.
- To be effective, feedback must be honest and delivered in the most appropriate time and place for the individual receiving the feedback.
- Lessen the impact of potentially difficult feedback by removing implied power and creating an environment where the other person is equal.
- The sandwich approach of delivering feedback opens by preparing the listener and providing positive comments before delivering constructive feedback. Close with a positive comment and/or encouragement.
- When you are the recipient of feedback, do not take it personally or become defensive. Listen, summarize the feedback to ensure you understand what was said, and thank the individual.

Call for Courage

Community Change

I was working at a table at our local farmer's market, supporting an initiative that was going on the following November's ballot. The first week, I was setting up our table when the man a few booths down was setting up his area. His table caught my attention because it was an opposing political affiliation to mine. I watched him talk to people and try to convince them to vote his way, and I felt the familiar stirring of bother inside me. I wondered if he knew about the cause I was supporting and was wishing I could share my view with him, but I was apprehensive about how he might respond. I saw him again over the next few weeks and since my purpose for being at the market was to get support for my cause, I finally found the courage to talk with him. To my surprise, it was a good conversation—not that he agreed with my point of view, but we were able to share our thinking with each other calmly. Rich and I had a conversation every Saturday about this initiative. I used humor and would often begin by asking him if he saw the light yet. He would laugh, and then we would talk. He asked questions and responded in a way that indicated his original thinking was being challenged. In the end, my courage to talk to him paid off when he said, "Tracy, I can honestly say that I don't know which way I'm going to vote now." I was so glad I found the courage to speak up.

Point of Courage: taking a risk talking about a politically charged issue, speaking up against injustice.

Chapter Four

RELATIONSHIPS: MAKING CONNECTIONS

"People don't care about how much you know until they know how much you care."

– Theodore Roosevelt

Introduction

Everything we do as leaders involves working with people, either directly or indirectly. The quality and authenticity of our relationships impacts the quality of our results—the stronger the relationship, the stronger the result. Part of the role of being a leader is about getting people aligned with the organization's vision and mission. Whether it's working with your team and internal staff or the partners of the organization, inspiring support is necessary to accomplish your goals. A leader who knows how to develop their team and keep them focused is essential to the success of the organization. Strong relationships play a vital part in a leader's ability to assist staff in developing their skills and motivate their effort.

I was most fortunate to work with a superintendent who, in his connection with me, modeled how developing an authentic relationship can impact results. From the first time I met Steve, I was drawn to his vision and ability to command a room by connecting with the people in it. To say that Steve was energetic is an understatement. His unbounded energy was infectious. Speaking from an organizational hierarchical context, as superintendent, Steve was at the top of the organization, and as the director of the child development department, I was much further down that chain. However, from our first meeting, Steve showed absolute respect for me. He sought out my ideas and listened when I spoke.

At one point, he asked me to lead an organizational project to explore the history of leadership in the district and make recommendations on how it informed our next steps. My workload was quite heavy, and I was already involved in several district-wide organizations and projects. When he approached me with that task, I was initially perplexed at how I could accomplish his request. However, because of the authentic connection he'd established with me over time and my respect for his leadership, I was motivated to figure it out. And figure it out I did. I learned to use more of my capacity and how to expand my efficiency. Rather than the project weighing me down and causing me stress, it energized me. I enjoyed the project and was able to give him the data he requested. I attribute that positive experience to the relationship Steve and I developed. Strong relationship, strong result!

The Importance of Relationships to Leaders

In real estate, they say the most important consideration is "location, location, location." In leadership, I consider the key component to be "relationships, relationships, relationships." Connecting with people and letting them know they are important is foundational to the success in any organization. Being authentic and sincere in those connections will build trust and help the relationship endure.

When we develop a deeper understanding of one another, it forms a bond that shifts our perspective of how we view each other. I believe relationships can be powerful beyond measure, so much so that I tell my clients that, "Connecting with others has the ability to transform our experience and create unprecedented results."

When I work with clients who have an executive team or cabinet as part of their structure, it is common for their subordinates to refer to decisions made by those groups as coming from "the execs" or "the cabinet." In this scenario, the people who make up the executive team or cabinet are objectified, rather than experienced for who they are as people. This also happens in organizations that are regulated by state or federal mandates. Again, when people in the organization talk about a situation, especially if it is negatively impacted by those mandates, I've heard things like, "The state says we have to ..." or "That's just the way it is because of the feds." By objectifying people, you separate out the humanness and create fodder for blanket criticism of them, not because of who they are, but because of the group they represent. Too often, apathetic paralysis to do things differently can set in. "The state" or "feds" or "execs" can sound larger than life. Conversely, if we refer to individuals by name, there is an element of humanness that facilitates approachability. People working in the organization are now more likely to develop the relationships with individuals that are necessary for interactions to occur at a deeper level.

If a leader desires to create authentic relationships, it is their responsibility to ensure that they are seen as people, not objects. I understand that it might be easier for some leaders to use the guise of allowing their decisions to come from "the execs, the state, or the feds" because there is some degree of vulnerability when seen as an individual who made the decision, rather than being part of a group. However, being vulnerable is a critical component necessary to develop trust in a relationship.

Four Cornerstones of Effective Relationships at Work

In my experience, the four components that are necessary to develop effective relationships are respect, trust, credibility, and give and take. Each component is foundational to creating and maintaining relationships necessary to build a successful organization.

Respect

Each person defines respect according to their belief about what respect means to them. How one defines respect is unique and is impacted by where they grew up and their culture and norms. In organizations, people tend to use the word respect as if everyone knows exactly what it means. While behaviors such as active listening, positive body language, and staying focused on the individual who is speaking are generally understood as signs of respect, some other behaviors fall into a gray area. In some cultures, maintaining direct eye contact can be considered disrespectful. Likewise, working on your laptop during a meeting while people are speaking can be considered disrespectful in some organizations, but not in others.

Remember, this chapter is about relationships. In regard to respect, being clear on how you define it is essential to avoid getting triggered if you feel "disrespected." It is also helpful to find out what is considered respectful to the other individuals in your group.

Example in Leadership:

I once believed that being on time was understood as a universal concept. If a meeting started at 8:00, it meant that everyone was in their seats ready to engage in the meeting at 8:00, not 8:01 or after. During weekly meetings, an individual I supervised always arrived about 10 minutes late. It really irritated me, and I felt disrespected. She was someone I otherwise respected and had a good relationship with, so rather than make a demand, I decided to ask her about it. She explained that in her culture, being a few minutes late was considered being on time. I was aghast; it didn't make any sense to me. I wanted to simply declare that meetings started at 8:00, period. However, after I got my indignation under control, we had a good discussion. I decided to talk about it with the group. Regardless of having different viewpoints on the subject, or that I was the leader and could have set the time, the fact that we got it out in the open preserved and even strengthened the relationship. I also learned that pausing to listen, rather than to react, was my opportunity to demonstrate the respect I was asking for. We ultimately agreed that everyone would be ready to begin the meeting at 8:00. The process of discussing the issue openly deepened the respect members had for me as their leader and also for their colleagues.

Can I develop a relationship with someone I don't respect?

Sometimes in business, we can't avoid working with people we don't respect. If you are in this situation, I recommend focusing on whatever common ground you can find. Relating on a professional level and concentrating on the task at hand may at least enable you to get the job done.

Trust

As the second component of developing relationships, trust ensures that people can count on you to say or do what you say you will. Trust is aligned with authenticity. With it, trust makes relationships genuine and lasting. Without it, leaders may be viewed as shallow, manipulative, and not worth listening to. Once trust is broken, it takes a long time to repair. Depending on what was violated, there are times when trust can never be restored. As a leader, it is imperative to understand the role of trust to avoid the possibility of damaging relationships.

Example in Leadership:

If a colleague or someone you supervise shares something with you in confidence and you don't honor that confidence, any trust they had in you may be called into question. Once doubt creeps in, the relationship begins to erode. If you don't take action to respond to that breech, the relationship bonds are broken.

What to do if trust is broken:

Apologize and take responsibility for violating the confidentiality. Being authentic in the interaction is essential. It has been my experience as a leader that when I've sincerely apologized, admitted my humanness, and committed to do better, it has been met with appreciation. I was given the benefit of the doubt and a chance to prove that I would "walk my talk" in the future.

Can I develop a relationship with someone I don't trust?

In this case, the relationship would be shallow at best, but more likely contentious. If there were no trust, doubt would be ever-present. I believe in giving people multiple chances to regain my trust; however, if someone has proven they can't be trusted, it may be necessary to sever the relationship.

Credibility

In Chapter Two, we discussed how credibility and authenticity are linked. If you are not authentic, you won't have any credibility in relationships. The other necessary component of credibility is subject matter competency. If you don't have the necessary knowledge in your field, you don't have credibility. Can you imagine going to a heart surgeon who has never been in the operating room? Or hiring a chef to fix your electrical problem? Of course not. Credibility has to do with believability, and that involves experience. Your proven abilities and consistent demonstration of competency definitely improve the likelihood that someone will respect and trust your knowledge and want to hear what you have to say. To establish credibility, say what you will do and then do it, every time.

Example in Leadership:

Hiring staff is an investment leaders make for their organization. The cost of staff turnover is high, both monetarily and in the negative impact it has on the morale of other staff. A candidate who says they're credible is very different from a candidate who demonstrates their credibility. I've worked with clients who have continual problems with high staff turnover. During our coaching sessions, I hear them say, "But he/she was so nice; they told us they knew how to do the work." I help my clients see that even though the candidates demonstrated believability with their verbal assurance, credibility was not established. Not only is credibility of the candidates at issue here, credibility of a leader to make the right hiring choices is also in question. If your staff sees that the new people you bring into an organization quickly leave or don't work out, you will hear them say things like, "I wonder how long he/she will last?" It may sabotage any chance the new person has to bond and leaves the rest of the staff feeling disheartened. When staff is discouraged or expressing cynicism, their work quality suffers.

If someone you hire ends up not having the skills they told you they had, you need to make a decision. Does the person have the ability to learn the skills they need quickly enough to do the job effectively? If so, create a learning plan and be sure to hold them accountable. If not, keeping them in the position will set them up for failure and will call your credibility as a leader into question.

Give and Take

A leadership role is a demanding position. Leaders who are "givers" feel the effects of those demands and quickly learn to set boundaries or face burnout. Leaders give of their time, their resources, and their talent. Many are overburdened and stretched thin. Leaders who are "takers" are seen as manipulative, lack credibility as competent leaders, and are not respected. Morale tends to be low, and the staff feels overworked or exploited.

For a relationship to be productive, balance between giving and taking is essential. As you get to know someone, you start to discover what you have to offer and what the other person has to offer. If one person in the relationship does all the giving or all of the taking, there will eventually be disappointment or resentment, which can lead to disintegration of the relationship. The most effective relationships are based on mutual benefit.

Example in Leadership:

I had a friend who could be counted on to do anything that was asked of her, and do it well. She wanted to be liked by everyone and was a classic example of a giver. Her boss was good at making demands without giving anything in return, a classic taker.

When her boss asked her to handle the disgruntled customers, she did it; go to every community meeting to represent the organization, whether during the week or weekend, she did it; stay late to finish a project, she did it.

Over time, I watched her become increasingly bitter and resentful of the fact that she missed her children's soccer games and music performances. She shared with me how much she was giving, and how now she felt taken advantage of and worn out. In desperation, she gave two weeks' notice that she was leaving the organization. Her boss feigned half-hearted disappointment at her resignation, which only added salt to the wound.

This situation didn't have to have an unhappy ending. On the part of my friend, being able to recognize the imbalance in her giving and the destructive effects of the false illusion that she was indispensable to the company could have made all the difference. This would have given her the opportunity to express her needs and set boundaries.

Her boss, the leader in this situation, could have equally shifted the tide if he had recognized his extreme in being a taker. He might have chosen to ask other employees to share the burden of those tasks or at the very least elicit a conversation with my friend to learn how she felt about doing all of the extra work.

Give and take requires self-confidence, humility, and daily practice. As a leader, giving can come in many forms: from giving of self in the form of an admission of wrongdoing to something more tangible like a simple acknowledgement, appreciation in words, a small token, or a raise. As a leader, taking can be mitigated by being flexible with an employee's schedule to acknowledgement, appreciation, or asking, rather than demanding, when you need the employee to do something.

Building effective relationships doesn't have to be difficult; it just takes both parties to give and take in balance.

Strategies to Cultivate a Positive, Lasting Relationship

There are a few strategies I've learned and used to help my relationships at work be productive and endure over time. In fact, these strategies, which have become a normal part of my authentic makeup, have resulted in many work relationships that have lasted over 25 years.

Share about yourself:

Letting others get to know you is one of the best ways to build relationships. Sharing your knowledge and expertise willingly can let people see you are approachable. This may feel vulnerable; however, as a leader, sharing your voice gives you an opportunity to develop credibility.

Focusing on the other person:

People generally like to know they are important to you; and when you focus on them, it conveys that message. Listening to learn and being curious about what someone else thinks about a given situation sends a signal that you value them. One point to consider here: as a leader, it is important to remember there is a power difference implicit in your position. When you focus on the other person, it could be perceived by some as an interrogation. By offering information about yourself and allowing the other person to focus on you, too, it creates a natural flow in the conversation and minimizes any misperception of your intent.

Transparency:

Being willing to be vulnerable, open, honest, and clear about expectations helps cultivate the kind of culture that leads to positive relationships. Leaders who are transparent foster a culture of trust with their employees. Employees don't appreciate being the last to hear about new initiatives or decisions, so keeping them in the loop helps them feel that they are a valued part of the organization.

Building rapport:

Rapport is when you develop a bond with someone and understand each other's feelings and ideas. Connections between people are established very quickly. You've probably heard,

"You never get a second chance to make a first impression." In fact, it is known that people form an opinion about us within the first few seconds of meeting. Think about when you meet someone for the first time. If they make eye contact, smile, and extend their hand for a friendly handshake, you begin to feel connected to them and rapport is established immediately.

Speak supportively about people in your work environment:

As a leader, people listen very closely to what you say. When you speak positively about everyone, you are modeling professionalism and show that you are a supportive leader. This not only strengthens existing relationships, but others will be attracted by your good nature and positivity and want to get to know you. Making negative or cynical comments about others creates mistrust in you as a leader. If you talk that way about others, employees will wonder what you are saying about them.

Boundaries:

Leaders set the tone of acceptable and unacceptable behavior in the workplace. Clearly defining and setting professional boundaries helps your staff function more effectively. When everyone in an organization knows the defined lines of behavior, they are less distracted by drama created when boundaries don't exist. As a leader, it is important to know your own boundaries. By modeling them, you will create a solid foundation for successful relationships to flourish. Also, modeling your own boundaries in a healthy way encourages your staff to do the same for themselves.

Boundaries cover many areas. You may set a boundary for how much of your personal life you want to share at work, the hours you work, or the expected professional tone of conversation in your work environment. Setting clear boundaries helps employees know where you stand and what is expected of them.

I've experienced both types of bosses in my career, one who set clear boundaries and one who had no boundaries. The message from the boss who set clear boundaries was that she was focused on our organization and totally available for us during the workday. She didn't share much about her personal life, and we respected her boundary. It never felt personal or inhibiting because she made sure to connect with us and demonstrate her caring in other ways.

The boss who didn't have boundaries in this area was someone who shared nearly everything without filter. The impact it had was that the team often felt uncomfortable knowing the level of details that were shared. Some even felt compelled to share their own personal details, which resulted in many meetings being off task, with minimal production and much frustration. Boundaries, when set in a healthy and respectful way, create a more safe and productive space.

Showing appreciation:

Showing appreciation is recognition that goes a long way in helping people feel valued. Verbal acknowledgement of a success or praising the work someone did is confirmation that you notice his or her good work. A handwritten note takes only a few minutes and strengthens the connection in a relationship. The key to showing appreciation is in authentic delivery. If you give too much praise, it can be quickly perceived as being given "lip service". That is, your mouth is saying the words, but there is no real feeling behind it. Staff may feel like you don't mean what you're saying or that you are trying to manipulate them. Show your appreciation authentically with body language that is congruent with the message. For verbal appreciation, eye contact, a smile, and a sincere tone will convey the authenticity of your message.

Following up and following through:

Following up on a conversation with a phone call or other electronic communication underscores the positive intent of an interaction. It keeps you connected with the other person.

Doing what you say you're going to do demonstrates your credibility and builds trust. When people can count on you to keep your word, strong relationships are easily formed.

EMOTIONAL INTELLIGENCE (EI)

Understanding the role of emotions and EI in your work environment is essential. People, including yourself, are human beings first and workers second. I have a friend who trains teachers who work with young children on how to respond to the emotions of three and four year olds. She tells them, "Emotions just are. They cannot be commanded or demanded away." So is true with emotions in adults. While we have reasoning skills that a four-year-old child doesn't have, when we don't know how to manage our emotions, they are in charge. Emotions are a powerful force. They influence how we act and react. Emotions can range from being happy and joyful to fearful, sad, or angry. In the work environment, the emotions that are considered most undesirable are fear or anger. Expressing those two emotions can be seen as weak or interfering with the work at hand and are met with displeasure. Since relationships are dependent on trust, respect, and credibility, angry outbursts can undermine those elements.

If we suppress emotions, it doesn't mean those emotions go away. When emotions are held inside, they often emerge at an inopportune time and in an exaggerated way.

When I was in my mid-20s, I worked for a boss who was prone to angry outbursts when anyone in his leadership team underperformed or questioned his decisions. I remember one conversation in particular when I was sitting in a circle with 10 to 15 of my colleagues. The boss was telling us we needed to get results in a specific way for the company. In my opinion and that of my colleagues, it was a demand that was unreasonable and would have demeaned the people we supervised. In my naiveté in being a young leader, I thought he would want to hear how his direction would have negative and unintended consequences. I was wrong. As his face grew red and the veins bulged out of his neck, he loudly screamed, "JUST DO IT!!"

Needless to say, I was embarrassed and felt like I had been run over by an 18-wheeler! I felt so sick in my stomach as I had to sit there and endure the stone cold silence in the room. My colleagues were stunned but felt so fearful that none of them dared to look in my direction. This interaction left effects that were felt by everyone in the room for weeks to follow. Colleagues expressed regret at not being able to say something for fear the boss's anger would be turned on them. It was difficult to re-focus on our work because much processing of "the incident" took center stage.

The example of a boss with very low EI demonstrates the effects from emotions unleashed and the devastating impact it can have, not only on the recipient of that emotion, but anyone else in the vicinity, as well.

What is EI?

Hendrie Weisinger, Ph.D. in *Emotional Intelligence at Work*, defines EI: "Quite simply, emotional intelligence is the intelligent use of emotions: you intentionally make your emotions work for you by using them to help you guide your behavior and thinking in ways that enhance your results."

Characteristics of Emotional Intelligence:

American psychologist Daniel Goleman developed a framework of five elements that define emotional intelligence.

Self-awareness

People with high EI are self-aware. They have the ability to recognize emotions in the moment and understand how different situations affect them emotionally. By understanding their emotions, they don't let their feelings rule them. They know their strengths and challenges and work on their challenges to improve their performance.

Self-regulation

Self-regulation is one's ability to control their emotions and impulses. People who self-regulate use their awareness to make choices on how to respond as to ensure a productive interaction. They typically don't allow themselves to react in extremes or to become overly angry. They don't make impulsive decisions, but think before they act.

Motivation

People with a high EI are willing to defer immediate results for long-term success. They are highly productive, love a challenge, and are effective in whatever they do.

Empathy

Empathy is the ability to identify with and understand the wants and needs of those around you. People with empathy are able to recognize the feelings of others, sometimes before the other person recognizes it. They detect subtle body language cues to inform their understanding of the communication.

Social skills

People with strong social skills are team players. Rather than focus on their own success, they help others develop and shine. They can manage disputes, are excellent communicators, and are masters at building and maintaining relationships.

Developing Emotional Awareness:

Develop a balcony view.

To increase your self-awareness, take a mental step back to observe yourself and develop your ability to have a balcony view. Having a balcony view means moving outside of yourself and reflecting on conversations and emotions you've had so you can assess and adjust them as necessary.

Make time for reflection.

In order to review or reflect on your interactions, it is necessary to carve out time in your day to focus on it. Making this part of your regular routine, at the end of your day before leaving the office or finding quiet time at home, will help you expand your awareness.

Increase your level of patience.

To increase your level of patience, you first need to be aware of when you are impatient. Keying into your own physiological responses, like increased heart rate, tapping your foot, or the tightening of your chest or stomach, will help you notice signs that could indicate nervousness. This information will allow you to respond by taking a moment to breathe more deeply, count to ten, or calm down your fidgeting.

Preserving a Relationship through a Difficult Time

Relationships go through difficult times, but that doesn't necessarily mean the relationship has to end. Going through a hard time with someone and getting to the other side can sometimes make the relationship stronger. By using the skills in Chapter Three on conflict resolution, leaders can become more comfortable with difficult conversations. It's important to be self-reflective and discover your role in that conversation. What could you have done differently? Remember, you can only be in control of you.

Improving relationships that are faltering.

If you feel that your relationship with someone is on rocky ground, the first thing to do is to identify why the relationship is faltering. Is it because of a negative interaction or lack of connecting?

If you've had a negative interaction, keep communication open. Reach out to the person and address the issue that is getting in the way. If you haven't connected lately, reach out and find time to reconnect.

Relationships are much like Wi-Fi. When there is a strong connection to the energy source, the signals are strong. If there is interference or static, you get a weak signal. Stay positively connected to your relationships, and they will serve you and your organization well.

REFLECTION ACTIVITY

Reflections to Strengthen Your Relationships

What does respect mean to you? Identify specific behaviors that you demonstrate to convey respect, as well as behaviors you expect from others that show respect.

How do your core values relate to or influence your work relationships?

Review the reflection lessons in Chapter Two on authenticity, and think about relationships in your life and the role that authenticity plays in them. What behaviors are most important for you to demonstrate your authenticity in a relationship?

What strengths of your communication style will you use to make your relationships more effective?

What skills will you develop to minimize the challenges that your communication style brings to a relationship?

Key Learning Points:

- Relationships are of utmost importance in leadership.
- Your communication with others has the ability to transform your experience and create unprecedented results.
- In order to create authentic relationships and cooperation, leaders must see others as people, not objects.
- Effective relationships must include: respect, trust, credibility, and give and take.
- To build or reestablish trust, be authentic. If you were wrong, admit it and apologize.
- Credibility requires authenticity, as well as subject matter competency. If you don't know what you don't know, your credibility and relationships will falter.
- In effective give and take, there is a balance and a mutual benefit. It is important to contribute what you can, without stretching your limits.
- You are more than a leader; you are a person. Be approachable and let others know who you are and what they can expect from you.
- Use the eight strategies in this chapter to create positive, lasting relationships.
- Increasing your emotional intelligence will enable you to use your emotions to strengthen, rather than destroy, relationships.

Call for Courage

Passing Grade

While teaching at a college in Baltimore, I wanted to change the grading system for students in my classes. I was told that it would most likely be very difficult to get the faculty and administration to accept my idea. I decided to move forward despite the concern because I felt it was the right thing to do for students. I solicited the help of one of my colleagues, who guided me through the process and gave me advice on what I would need to increase my chances of being successful. I prepared my talk just as my colleague advised, and when the day came to present my case, I was very nervous. When I stood up to speak, I felt my heart pounding and my face becoming flush. However, I knew I was prepared and my supportive colleague was sitting close by. To find the courage to speak, I focused on my presentation. In the end, the faculty and administration did agree to allow me to change the grading system. I attribute my relationships with colleagues and my commitment to doing the right thing as the basis for my courage.

Point of Courage: Pushing through my nervousness and talking in front of my peers, taking a risk.

Chapter Five

PERSONAL WELLNESS

In the event of a loss in cabin pressure, put the oxygen mask on yourself first!

ANYONE WHO HAS flown on a plane knows this instruction well. Without our own ability to breathe, we are of little help to anyone else. Leaders are famous for putting themselves last. From my own experiences as a leader and working with many clients, personal wellness is often an after-thought. Leaders tend to focus on the mission of their organization so intently, and thinking of themselves isn't even on their list of priorities. In the book *Leaders Eat Last*, the author states, "The true price of leadership is the willingness to place the needs of others above your own. Great leaders truly care about those they are privileged to lead and understand that the true cost of the leadership privilege comes at the expense of self-interest." I do agree that his point is well taken when considering others in some practices or decision making; though the importance of self-interest in self-care is of utmost importance for leaders to sustain high-quality effort.

My Wellness Journey

My early interest in personal health led me to pursue a degree in Health and Physical Education, where I learned all about the mechanics of the body and general health practices. I moved to California to accept a teaching position in San Francisco and taught high school students the value of health and physical education. I was immersed in my subject and walked my talk, modeling by taking good care of myself.

My first entrée into the concept of wellness was when I taught at the College of Note Dame in Baltimore a few years later. The administration asked me to teach a "comprehensive health course;" and in doing research for that course, I was introduced to an expanded version of health, called wellness. It was the first time I heard about the importance of the mind, body, and spirit connection. I continued to teach and facilitate workshops on wellness for the next 20 years. I taught about exercising, healthy eating, and the importance of taking care of the mind. I thought I had a good understanding of how to optimize personal health, but often found myself exhausted and restless.

As a typical "overachiever," I saw myself as limitless and was always looking for greater challenges. I moved back to California and happily accepted a leadership position in a school district in Sacramento. In my fifth year in that position, I decided it was time to take on an additional challenge, so I entered the doctoral program at the University of La Verne. The demands on my time were off the chart. Waking up at 4 am to study and putting in a 50-hour workweek was my regular cycle. Two years later, I was promoted and became director of the department, which expanded my leadership role to overseeing 350 staff. My 50-hour workweek quickly grew to 60 hours, and school studies took up the majority of my weekends. But at the time, I was young, healthy, and determined to "do it all." I made it through and earned my degree, but not without a toll on my body and mind. I was so immersed in school and work that I had minimal time for family and no time for friends. When I finished school, my body felt like I was still on a high-speed rail train. I had a hard time integrating back into my circle of friends. I remember someone asking me what I did for fun, and I couldn't come up with an answer. I was definitely out of balance.

During the next eight years, I continued to lead the department through many changes. I thought I was taking good care of myself, and maybe compared to many others, I was. Then, the stress from unreasonable demands at work began to mount. I was so focused on putting my energy into work, I had no awareness of my health. My body was screaming at me in the form of fatigue and chronic shoulder tension. I got every cold germ circulating and was seeing my doctor frequently. I was also seeing a massage therapist regularly, and the knots in my shoulders were so tight she couldn't get them to relax. It got so bad that I wasn't able to turn my head without extreme pain. My physical therapist put kinesio tape on my neck to help reduce the inflammation. I actually went to work taped from my shoulder to my neck for nearly a year. Here I was, someone with a degree in health who had been a teacher of wellness for 20 years, walking around with my neck taped, wincing in pain, and somehow still not recognizing that I needed to make a change! I can't say I put myself last, because I was so blind to my needs that I didn't even make myself part of the equation.

When my body, mind, and spirit finally broke down, I realized I had a choice to make: change my situation or face a much more serious health catastrophe. I made the change, took care of myself, and over the following two years, I slowly started to regain my health and balance.

What is Wellness?

Definitions and interpretations of wellness vary. Essentially, wellness is a comprehensive approach to self-care. Wellness is not an end-point; it's a way of living. It's a choice and a process, an integration of mind, body, and spirit, and it's personal to each one of us.

Examples of the range of definitions of wellness:

*"Wellness is the complete **integration** of body, mind, and spirit – the realization that everything we do, think, feel, and believe has an effect on our state of well-being."*

– Greg Anderson

*"Wellness is a **choice**, a way of life, a process, an efficient channeling of energy, an integration of mind, body, spirit, and a loving acceptance of self."*

– John Travis

*"It is a positive approach that implies **self-motivated** action. It implies the application of knowledge and information. The facts alone do not lead to a wellness life."*

– Bill Hetler

*"Wellness is a **conscious**, self-directed, and **evolving** process of achieving full potential."*

– Judd Allan, PhD

*"Wellness is a **process** of becoming aware of and making choices toward a more successful existence."*

– The National Wellness Institute

Each of the definitions call out a specific nuance. The words that stand out most clearly to describe wellness are integration, choice, self-motivated, conscious, evolving, and process.

Why is Wellness Important for Leaders?

Wellness is important for everyone. Leaders are confronted with demanding issues every day. From personal experience and that of my clients, the physical, emotional, and mental strain of being a leader takes an enormous toll on health. The ability to respond, make sound decisions, and have positive interactions is more likely when leaders are well fueled physically, mentally, emotionally, and spiritually. Conditions in organizations often shift dramatically from one day to the next, and a leader who is balanced in their wellness is much better able to respond and adapt.

People look to leaders as role models and are influenced by what they say and do. A leader who takes care of her/himself demonstrates that wellness is important. Conversely, a leader who doesn't value wellness sets the stage for an unhealthy work culture.

I once worked for a boss who considered it a badge of honor to work until late into the evening. During meetings with the leadership team, the boss would inevitably start the conversation talking about working late into the evening the night before. My colleagues and I internalized that message, and we found ourselves working late or feeling guilty if we left "on time." Being "on time" to some of us meant arriving long before 8:00 and leaving after 5:00 without taking any breaks. We all knew that the schedules we were keeping were not healthy or conducive to the kind of focused work we needed to do to maintain high quality. When we were able to take a vacation, it was not uncommon for us to spend it being sick. Our bodies were breaking down, our minds were exhausted, and our spirits dulled. It wasn't until after the boss left the department that we started to call out the unhealthy pattern and were able to institute a new culture of taking better care of ourselves. It took some time to shed the old feeling of guilt, but the results in increased work quality and production reinforced that it was the right thing to do.

Mind, Body, Spirit – From Disconnection to Connection

My early understanding of mind, body, and spirit was that each area was encapsulated in its own arena. I thought of each as a separate unit. I primarily focused on exercise, healthy foods, and cultivated my intellect. Integrating the three areas never occurred to me. Education and learning generally came easy to me, so my intellect was often in charge. When I was in balance, I listened to my inner voice; however, when I was out of balance, my mind was the ruler, dictating every decision. When I had a problem to solve, I went right to my head for a consult. After I had the breakdown of my body and spirit, I learned one of the most important lessons of my life:

"Don't let your intellect get in the way of your wisdom."

– Tracy Tomasky

It happened one evening a few weeks after I had gone through an extremely difficult experience. I was invited to a dinner where there would be a group of people who would undoubtedly be lamenting about the grueling experience. I felt compelled to go, but I also felt sluggish and resistant. A voice inside me resisted the message from my mind and encouraged me to listen to the other parts of myself. I had a profound experience as I heard myself say, "Okay, body and spirit, do you want to go to this dinner?" When I actually heard a loud internal "NO," I thought to myself, "Huh, I guess my mind was overruled 2-1." As soon as I decided I wouldn't go, I felt such a wave of relief and could almost hear my body and spirit cheering. That was an insightful experience and a true realization that our mind, body, and spirit each have their own voice that helps keep us in optimum health and balance.

Mind

"Our subconscious minds have no sense of humor, play no jokes, and cannot tell the difference between reality and an imagined thought or image. What we continually think about eventually will manifest in our lives."

– Sidney Madwed

Our minds are more powerful than we often realize. We can use our minds to recall memories that happened decades ago or transport us to whatever far reaching visions we create. Walt Disney used his mind to envision the "happiest place on earth." In Disneyland, we are immersed in the wonderment of his thinking. Great minds discovered cures for diseases and every invention we use today.

In Chapter One, we learned how our beliefs are formed in our subconscious mind and influence our present behavior. Beliefs are thoughts that we keep thinking; and by using our mind, we have the ability to change our beliefs. Consider the reframing examples on conflict we used in Chapter Three. If you believe conflict is difficult and never results in anything good, it will indeed be your reality. Use the power of your mind to transform that belief. By reframing your view of conflict as a good thing that gets us to the best solutions, you can replace the old belief with one that is more empowering.

Leaders tend to be knowledgeable and often rely on their intellect, which puts them out of balance. It's important to pay careful attention to what you allow into your mind, what you read, watch, and expose yourself to. I recall a close friend who regularly watched the evening news, read the local newspaper, and listened to talk radio from sources who were convinced the world was in horrible shape. He detailed every negative event on every show. He became more disgruntled, angry, and negative and found no joy in daily life. His wife strongly encouraged him to turn off the TV, give up the newspaper, and change what he listened to. As a couple, they replaced the news by watching old movies, listening to jazz music, instead of an over-abundance of political talk shows, and adventured out to local coffee houses to listen to live music. The change in him was remarkable. He transformed himself from a grouchy, surly, pessimistic guy to a thoughtful and joyful man who was fun to be around. He amazed even himself, and his relationship with his wife grew ever stronger.

Reflection Questions:

What sources of media, etc., do I engage in currently that are not contributing to having a healthy and positive mind?

What changes can I make in what I read, watch, and listen to that would be a positive influence in how I think and act?

Empowerment thought – I choose my thoughts and what I allow into my mind wisely.

Body

"You will receive one body, of which should you wear it out, you will have nowhere to live. You are expected to make alterations, improvements, and maintenance on a regular basis. How you feed and care for your body is paramount in how long you will operate at maximum efficiency."

– John Amaro

To help our bodies operate at maximum efficiency, we need to consider movement, nutrition, and rest. Our bodies need appropriate care and will respond to the level of care given. If we want optimal performance, we need to work with our body so it works with us.

Movement

I prefer to use the term movement, rather than exercise, because it is more motivating for people. For some people, the word exercise elicits groans and thoughts of dragging oneself around a track or gym. Movement is what our body is designed to do.

Simple changes in our habits can make a difference in establishing new patterns of movement. For example, take the stairs instead of an elevator or park in a space farther from the entrance. There are also secondary gains in the parking example. Not only will you have the benefit of taking extra steps, you won't have the stress of driving around and around a parking lot or competing with a car coming from the other direction to get that closest space.

Leaders spend a lot of time in meetings. Including "walking meetings" is a great way to add movement and get some fresh air at the same time. I used this practice in some of my meetings and fondly recall one of my administrators who during times of high stress would say to my assistant, "It's time to walk the Director," and away we'd go. Walking out the stress and having a meeting resolving issues, too, always left me feeling better and more productive.

The many benefits of movement include:
- increased energy level
- weight management
- promotes better sleep
- prevents loss of bone density

- decreases stress
- elevates mood
- improves cognition

According to the Mayo Clinic (www.mayoclinic.org), the general rule is to aim for 30 minutes of physical activity every day. If you have other specific fitness goals, it is important to check with your doctor before starting any new exercise program.

Empowerment thought – My body is designed to move, and I feel better when I move!

Nutrition

When we think about nutrition, it is too often synonymous with the word "diet." To me, the word diet has a negative connotation, bringing up feelings of lack and deprivation. I find that by reframing my thinking of nutrition from being on a diet to viewing eating as fuel for my body, I make much better choices about what I eat.

For most of my life, I was very thin. I began to put on a few extra pounds each year, to the point that I weighed 30 pounds more than was comfortable for my small 5'2" frame. I felt tired and sluggish most of the time. I got tired of feeling tired and was motivated to make a change. At that time, I worked in a culture that loved food. On any given day, one could walk past the break area and find delicious cookies, cupcakes, donuts, cheesy dips, etc. I couldn't go near that area without indulging. I even played the game of "I'll just have half of a cookie," only to go back for another bite since, after all, I was only eating half of that cookie. I finally realized that it was habit, not really even wanting the cookie that guided my choice to eat it mindlessly. I made the first change that became a strategy that worked for me then, and I still use today.

I decided that when I walked past the food, I would pause, look at the food, and ask myself, "Do you really want that?" If I did want it, I ate it and enjoyed every bit without imposing guilt on myself. Increasingly, I found that when I asked myself the question, the answer was, "No, I really don't." I was able to easily walk past the food that had previously called my name.

I made a few other changes in how I fueled my body. I increased fresh fruits and vegetables, decreased my bread and sugar intake, and kept a glass of water close at hand. Staying hydrated was the most important strategy, so I didn't confuse hunger with actually being thirsty. I ate three smaller meals with two healthy snacks in between. These small changes shifted how I thought about food. My new pattern of eating also infused and fueled my body with lasting energy, instead of being fooled by the short-term energy blasts of sugar and caffeine.

I want to acknowledge that food issues can be deep seated and intertwined with emotional issues or messages we got about food when we were young. I in no way intend to make this sound like it is an easy process or right for anyone else. I reiterate that it is important to check with your doctor before adopting a new eating plan.

Empowerment thought – I choose food that will fuel me for maximum performance.

Rest

If I ask most leaders about the role that rest plays in their lives, the response most assuredly will be, "Rest, what's that?" Leaders are the "can do" and work until the work is done kind of people. Clients tell me that they can't rest, they just have too much to do. I also hear more flippant comments like, "I'll rest when I'm dead." The truth is that when we allow our bodies to rest, we are able to relax. If we are tightly wound with our bodies and mind in constant motion, there isn't time or space for creative energy to flow. It is from a relaxed state that we are able to be most productive. For those of you who naturally move at a fast pace, being relaxed doesn't have to mean slow movement. It has more to do with an inner calm, more centered way of being.

Think about when you go on vacation or take time off. Are you able to relax from day one? If so, you are most likely in balance. If you're like me when I'm in work mode, it takes a few days or more to finally be able to feel the relaxation set in. Think about this scenario:

A typical leader from the baby boomer generation works a hurried and harried schedule, moving at the speed of light for 48 to 50 weeks a year. He/she gets 2 to 3 weeks of vacation spread out over the year. Weekends are crammed with family and friends, interspersed with checking emails or work-related phone calls. I had one client say that his life feels like one giant hamster wheel.

What if you reframed your concept of rest and relaxation? Schedule in a 10-minute rest period in your day and time for yourself on weekends. Before you tell me that finding even 10 minutes is impossible, I invite you to consider making a commitment and looking at it this way, "I will schedule 10 minutes for myself every day." Then find the time and schedule it.

"Whether you think you can or you think you can't, you're right."

– Henry Ford

<u>Empowerment thought</u> – Getting the rest and relaxation I need will make me more productive.

Reflection Questions:

What messages in my early years did I receive about movement, eating, and rest?

What beliefs about movement, eating, and rest do I want to change?

Spirit

"Enlightened leadership is spiritual if we understand spirituality not as some kind of religious dogma or ideology but as the domain of awareness where we experience values like truth, goodness, beauty, love and compassion, and also intuition, creativity, insight and focused attention."

– Deepak Chopra

Of the three dimensions of wellness, spirit is the most personal. For the purposes of this book and the role of spirit in wellness, I will refer to spirit simply as a connection to a higher source, whether it be God, another deity, nature, or other connection that is right for you. It is important to note that I am talking about spirit in a broad context, not in the context of religion. I make no judgment of anyone's belief, religious or otherwise. I hold true that everyone has the right to be "right" regarding how they believe and how they apply their beliefs to *their own life.*

I think of spirit as my heart center that connects me to a universal energy. My QiGong teacher taught from a philosophy that referred to our hearts as our heart-mind. This reference implies that our heart has an intelligence of its own. Engaging our spirit is the result of using our heart to inform our thinking. When we listen to the answer, we are tapping into our intuition; and in that way, we have our own internal navigation system. I have learned to engage my spirit in my decisions, and the results I get when I do are exceptional. I can tell the difference when I use my mind exclusively and forget my spirit in an interaction or decision because I feel disconnected, out of alignment.

Choosing to follow the guidance of your spirit can sometimes feel uncomfortable because it can take you out of your comfort zone. It is at the crossroads of choosing between letting your intuition guide you and retreating in fear that authenticity can be anchored.

Spirituality and Religion – A Not-So-Merry Holiday

In the workplace, there are times that spirituality and religion are in conflict. As leaders, there may be people we supervise who have different and sometimes opposing beliefs when it comes to spirituality or religion. I experienced this firsthand as a new leader. There were 70 staff in our administrative office. The issue of spiritual or religious beliefs was especially contentious during the month of December. Upon entering the front door, the office was transformed into all things red and green and other representations of Christmas. Of the 70 staff members in the office, two were Jewish, one was Jehovah Witness, one Wiccan, and the rest were Christian. The voices of the minority groups were silent, but two of them confided in me about how hurtful it felt to them to feel invisible and excluded. I was faced with a dilemma as the new leader. Do I just sympathetically nod and share how sorry I was, or do I acknowledge that there was an injustice going on and address the problem?

I didn't struggle with the decision for long. I consulted my inner guidance and checked in with my core value of respect and the organization's espoused value of inclusivity. I ignited my courage and decided to tackle what I knew would not be an easy process. I took the perspective that we were in a work environment, everyone mattered, and we needed to find some balance. I articulated my message clearly that in our office of 70, "The 1 is as important as the other 69."

Initially the dominant group responded with statements like, "Well, they are welcome to put their menorah on their desk," and "You can't tell me I can't wear my Christmas sweater." I even had one person write a letter to the Governing Board complaining that Tracy Tomasky doesn't like Santa Claus. Seriously, if they could only see my house at Christmas!

Since this was a work environment and inclusivity was a value of the organization, the new guidelines prohibited excessive Christmas decorations, especially in the areas where customers entered. Down came the Christmas trees, red and green paper chains, and jingle bells strewn all across the office. Less ostentatious decorations were allowed in each desk area. I also encouraged conversation with each other to learn about celebrations other than their own. I had to work through some very high emotions and tough conversations during that time, but I never moved off my message of the importance of respect and inclusivity. It took about five years to find some balance, and there always remained an undercurrent of frustration, especially as December approached each year. The four people who originally felt invisible shared with me their appreciation and how good they felt to know that they mattered. Hearing that they felt valued was worth every effort and difficult conversation I went through to help change the culture to be more inclusive. In the depths of my being, I knew I had done the right thing.

Benefits of a Higher Source Connection

There are great benefits to being connected to a higher source. The feeling of not being alone but that you have a "support team" brings about more confidence, focus, and strength. Whenever fear starts to creep in, it is my connection to my higher source that ignites my pilot light of courage. As a leader, that has been invaluable to me. During difficult times, my higher source has offered guidance or a soft place to land when things didn't go well. During good times, the connection to my higher source lets me know that I am aligned with my spirit.

Developing Your Connection

Developing your higher source connection helps you be a stronger leader. This connection is personal, unique to you. Strategies to help you develop a connection with a higher source:

- Develop your awareness of when, and in what settings, you feel most connected to your inner self.
  - Is it when you are in nature, a place of worship, or other location?
  - What does your environment look like when you feel most connected? What is the noise level in the room? What is the lighting like?
- Get comfortable with quiet. This is an area that can be difficult for people who are accustomed to being in a noisy environment. These suggestions can feel uncomfortable at first but can make a positive impact with practice.
  - turn the radio off while driving – if this feels like too big of a challenge, try lowering the volume over time.

- turn your TV off unless you are intentionally watching a program you are interested in (rather than keeping it on for background noise).
- remove distractions from your environment that cause you to be in "doing" mode.
- Spending time in nature
    - nature can be found everywhere – in the woods, in a park, by the ocean, in your neighborhood, or backyard. Connect with the nature around you through awareness and gratitude.
- Attend a church, synagogue, mosque, or other place of spiritual practice
- Meditate
- Practice gratitude daily: Practicing gratitude regularly has significant benefits. People who practice gratitude tend to:

Experience more positive emotions	Express more compassion and kindness
Have a stronger immune system	Recognize and enjoy life's small pleasures
Have lower anxiety	Experience fewer aches and pains
Feel a sense of abundance	Have improved psychological health – mental strength
Sleep better	Feel less lonely

Reference: Greatergood.berkeley.edu

Reflection Questions:

What messages did you receive in your early years regarding spirituality and/or religion?

How are you integrating those messages in your life currently? Are the spiritual/religious beliefs you practice consistent with your core values?

Empowerment thought – I have everything I need to access my inner wisdom.

How do I make myself priority?

Reflection on Priorities

What are the top three things that you give priority to in your life currently?

1.
2.
3.

If "you" are not listed as #1, or even among the top 3, what makes the others more important than you?

1.
2.
3.

What is getting in your way of making yourself priority #1?

1.
2.
3.

What are the top three things you could do to take care of yourself?

1.

2.

3.

If you took care of these top three areas for yourself, how would you feel?

1.

2.

3.

As a leader, what positive message would you be sending to those around you if you made yourself priority #1?

1.

2.

3.

What steps will you take to ensure that you make yourself priority one?

1.

2.

3.

Lead by Example – Make Yourself Priority One!

The Role of Stress

The top three findings in a study done by The Center for Creative Leadership reveal that:

88% of leaders report that work is a primary source of stress in their lives and that having a leadership role increases the level of stress.

More than 60% of surveyed leaders cite their organizations as failing to provide them with the tools they need to manage stress.

More than two-thirds of surveyed leaders believe their stress level is higher today than it was five years ago.

My own experience as a leader and in working with clients who are in leadership roles confirms the negative impact that stress plays. Looking for coaching and strategies to manage stress is another top issue my clients bring to me. As leaders, they are dealing with difficult personnel issues, making tough decisions, working long hours, managing competing priorities, trying to balance diminishing budgets and a myriad of other complex aspects of their jobs. They feel pulled between their homes and their office. They don't have enough time in the day, and they feel stressed!

Now take a breath—there is much you can do to reframe how you view stress, prevent stress, and respond to it.

Gerald G. Jampolsky, MD offers a powerful statement about stress,

"It's not the situation that's causing your stress, it's your thoughts, and you can change that right here and now. You can choose to be peaceful right here and now. Peace is a choice, and it has nothing to do with what other people do or think."

Now if it were only that easy. Maybe it is …

What is Stress?

Stress is a normal physical response to events that make you feel threatened or upset your balance in some way. It is your body's "fight-or-flight" reaction. Whether it's real or imagined, your perception is your reality. Stress is also your body's way of protecting you.

Benefits of Stress

Believe it or not, stress has real benefits. Beneficial stress is called eustress. The term was coined by endocrinologist Hans Selye. Eustress is of Greek origin and is made up of "Eu," meaning good and stress. Eustress is literally "good stress." A certain amount of stress is necessary for you to stay focused, energetic, and alert. In emergency situations, it gives you extra strength to defend yourself or help others. Think about stories of someone being able to lift a car off of someone. Stress can help you rise to meet challenges. If giving a speech or presentation makes you feel nervous, just the right amount of stress helps you to stay sharp and focused.

Harmful Stress

When you have too much stress or constant stress over time, it can cause major damage to your health, productivity, relationships, and quality of life. By understanding the causes, signs, and unhealthy responses to stress, you are better prepared to develop your toolbox of strategies to minimize stress's effects.

Causes of Stress

There are many causes of stress, both external and internal. External stress can include major life changes, financial problems, relationship difficulties, work, and family issues. Internal stress can include an inability to accept uncertainty, negative self-talk, and having unrealistic expectations.

Signs of Stress

Stress shows up differently for each of us, and signs might include body aches, forgetfulness, tight muscles, poor judgment, feeling tired, an inability to concentrate, or having trouble sleeping. Being easily irritated, constantly worrying, or unprovoked outbursts of anger may also be signs of stress.**

**The signs noted about stress may also be from other causes, and it is recommended that you see your health practitioner for appropriate assessment.

Common Unhealthy Responses to Stress

When we are under stress, it is not uncommon to be unaware of how we are responding. Stress clouds our thinking. For example, someone under stress may engage in excessive eating or drinking alcohol to calm down, speak or eat very fast, work extra-long hours, sleep too much or too little, or procrastinate and not get anything done.

Developing a Toolbox of Strategies to Minimize the Effects of Stress

There are definite advantages to preventing stress. Imagine being able to calmly move throughout your day, regardless of the number of problems that come your way, or starting your day with energy that lasts through the day. By developing and following a personal wellness plan, stress will have new meaning for you. It will no longer hold you in its grip or dictate your actions, and it will have less chance of harming your wellbeing. The following strategies offer suggestions for preventing and responding to stress as it shows up in your life.

Stress Prevention Strategies:

- Establish a personal wellness plan
- Develop a strong support system – spend quality time with family and friends to nurture your relationships

- Engage in a daily meditation or relaxation routine:
  - Sit in a comfortable position with your feet on the floor and your hands in your lap or lie down. Close your eyes.
  - Picture yourself in a peaceful place. Perhaps you're lying on the beach, walking in the mountains or floating in the clouds. Hold this scene in your mind.
  - Inhale and exhale. Focus on breathing slowly and deeply.
  - Continue to breathe slowly. Start with 5 minutes and extend it over time.
- Keep a daily gratitude journal
- Learn to say no and set healthy boundaries
- Manage your time – pace yourself, don't over-schedule
- Develop a system of organization at home and at work
- Leave work at work
- Learn to accept the things you cannot change
- Set your watch 5 to 10 minutes ahead to avoid the stress of being late
- Get out of your own way – strive for excellence over perfectionism, done is better than perfect

Strategies for Responding to Stressful Situations:

In the immediate moment of a stressful interaction:
- Count to 10 before you speak
- Take 3 to 5 deep breaths
- Walk away from the stressful situation, and say you'll handle it later
- Go for a walk

Change strategies for longer-term stressful environments
- Slow down
- Replace worry with a positive thought

- Nurture yourself
- Remember to laugh
- Break down big problems into smaller parts
- Drive in the slow lane or avoid busy roads to help you stay calm while driving
- Resolve conflict positively
- Don't hesitate to say "I'm sorry" if you make a mistake
- Delegate activities you don't enjoy whenever possible
- Use employer-sponsored benefits, i.e., flex hours, a compressed work week, job sharing
- Positive self-talk:
  - "I will do the best I can."
  - "I can handle things if I take one step at a time."
  - "I know how to deal with this; I've done it before."
  - "I can get help if I need it."
  - "We can work it out."
  - "I won't let this problem get me down."
  - "I'm human, and we all make mistakes."
  - "Someday I'll laugh about this."

Stress Relief - Do Something Fun or Relaxing:

- Take a walk in nature
- Listen to music
- Have coffee/tea with friends
- Start a new hobby
- Read a favorite book or magazine
- Engage in a sport you enjoy
- Watch an old movie that has positive meaning to you
- Learn something new—cooking or photography

Reframe: The power of language and thought to reduce stress

Powerless: "My life often feels out of control."

Empowering: "I can't always control what happens in my life, but I can control how I respond to it."

Powerless: "I have to give a talk tomorrow, and I'm scared out of my mind."

Empowering: "I have to give a talk tomorrow, and I'm a little nervous. I'll do my best, and it will all turn out just fine."

Stress Prevention Management Plan

The following tool can be used to develop strategies to prevent stress and cultivate calm and balance in your life.

Stress Prevention Management Plan

Strategy I want to develop	Resources Needed	Specific activities to reinforce the strategy	Timeline to implement specific activity	Check-In time for status of completion
Example: Begin a gratitude journal	Purchase a journal	Wake up 15 min. earlier to write in my journal	Daily beginning …	Every Sunday

Where Do I Start?

After taking the wellness assessment at the end of the chapter, complete the reflection questions.

In preparing to develop your Personal Wellness Plan, review the foundational concepts in this next section. There are six components that I have experienced to be the most successful in developing a wellness plan: the *obstacle dump*, developing *awareness* of a positive *mindset* and motivation strategies, *focus* on the area where you want to make change, *commitment* to your plan, *accountability,* and *celebrating* your results.

The Obstacle Dump

This technique is one of my favorite and most successful strategies for preparing yourself to learn something new, increase your awareness, or let go of anything that is not serving you.

1. Set a timer for three minutes.
2. On a piece of paper, write down all of the things that are weighing heavy   on your mind or getting in your way. Don't think or analyze anything you are writing, follow your stream of consciousness.
3. After three minutes, tear up the paper into pieces and throw them in a trash can.
4. Take a deep breath.
5. Now you are ready to proceed with your wellness planning.

Awareness

Adopting a "possibility" mindset for change is necessary to accomplish anything. You must believe that the condition you desire can happen or the change cannot occur. What you believe will be your reality.

Motivation:

Knowing what motivates you to take action will help support your plan.
- working with a partner
- setting goals
- rewarding yourself
- having a routine
- journaling

What obstacles to your motivation get in your way?

In what ways can you eliminate or minimize those obstacles?

Focus

Choose the area you want to work on and make a specific plan for change. By focusing your energy on one area, you will minimize distractions.

"Effort and courage are not enough without purpose and direction."

– JFK

Commitment

The first step to making a commitment is to declare your action to yourself. Some people find it helpful to share their commitment with others as a means of establishing accountability. I have found that commitments that have realistic expectations are most helpful in fulfilling the commitment. Small wins are motivating. See the specific steps in the Personal Wellness Plan section later in this chapter.

Accountability

Accountability to yourself is about taking responsibility to implement your personal wellness plan. Checking in regularly to assess your progress will help you stay focused on your plan.

"Accountability breeds response-ability." -Stephen Covey

Celebration

Celebrating the milestones you set for yourself along the way can be highly motivating. Celebrating along the way also reminds us of the importance of the journey.

I will celebrate my successes by:

Every journey begins with a single step...

Wellness Questionnaire

This questionnaire is designed to give you a sense of how you see yourself in eight areas. It is a brief snapshot of your current life in time. There are no judgments of right/wrong, good/bad. It is intended to be a tool to assist you in creating the life you want.

Please respond to the following statements with either "true" or "false." If the statement is true usually or all of the time for you, mark "true." If the statement is seldom or never descriptive of you, mark "false." After completing the questionnaire, tally the number of "true responses" and fill out the Evaluation of your Wellness Assessment.

EMOTIONAL

T_____ F_____ I am willing to see a mental health counselor for emotional concerns.

T_____ F_____ When I need to, I can say "no" without feeling guilty.

T_____ F_____ I seldom "lose control" when I'm angry.

T_____ F_____ I am happy most of the time.

T_____ F_____ I have a number of people in my life who I care for and who care for me.

T_____ F_____ I can share with others my feelings and concerns easily.

T_____ F_____ I often feel "stressed out."

T_____ F_____ I am not embarrassed by, or afraid of, other people's emotions.

T_____ F_____ I consider my friends positive people, rather than negative people.

T_____ F_____ I feel good about who I am.

Total # of True responses:_____

PHYSICAL

T_____ F_____ I am aware of the quality and quantity of foods I eat.

T_____ F_____ I do not smoke or use tobacco products.

T_____ F_____ I do not get sick more than once or twice a year.

T_____ F_____ I exercise moderately or better at least three times per week.

T_____ F_____ I can fall asleep easily and sleep through the night.

T_____ F_____   I drink the equivalent of 8 glasses of water every day.

T_____ F_____   I have plenty of energy.

T_____ F_____   Fruits and vegetables are a significant part of my diet.

T_____ F_____   I'm not dependent on drugs (other than those needed for medical conditions).

T_____ F_____   I do some form of stretching exercise at least twice a week.

Total # of True responses:_____

INTELLECTUAL

T_____ F_____   I enjoy learning new skills and information.

T_____ F_____   I trust my ability to make good decisions.

T_____ F_____   I feel that I can see more than one side of an issue.

T_____ F_____   I can clearly explain to others what I know about something.

T_____ F_____   I keep informed about world issues and events.

T_____ F_____   I have many creative ideas.

T_____ F_____   I am comfortable expressing myself publicly.

T_____ F_____   I commit time and energy to professional growth and self-development.

T_____ F_____   I am aware that my environment influences my thoughts.

T_____ F_____   I use my thoughts to make my reality more positive.

Total # of True responses:_____

SPIRITUAL

T_____ F_____ I take time for spiritual growth and exploration.

T_____ F_____ I have a belief in a higher power.

T_____ F_____ My life has direction and meaning.

T_____ F_____ I take time to think about the meaning of events in my life.

T_____ F_____ I have a clear sense of right and wrong.

T_____ F_____ I feel comfortable talking about my spiritual needs.

T_____ F_____ I am able to explain why I believe what I believe.

T_____ F_____ I generally live my life in a way that reflects my values.

T_____ F_____ I have a general sense of peace and calm.

T_____ F_____ I care about what happens to others.

Total # of True responses:_____

SOCIAL

T_____ F_____ I have friends with whom I can participate in activities I enjoy.

T_____ F_____ I have a sense of belonging to a group or organization.

T_____ F_____ I am not afraid to go to places where I might not know anyone.

T_____ F_____ I value time alone.

T_____ F_____ People enjoy being with me.

T_____ F_____ I feel that I have "enough" friends.

T_____ F_____ I generally like people, and people generally like me.

T_____ F_____ I can go to a party and have a good time.

T_____ F_____   I feel that I have a good sense of humor.
T_____ F_____   I am able to set my boundaries and respect the boundaries of others.

Total # of True responses:_____

WORK/MONEY

T_____ F_____   I am generally satisfied with my vocation.
T_____ F_____   My work is stimulating and rewarding.
T_____ F_____   I believe that I am a valuable employee.
T_____ F_____   I am proud of my accomplishments.
T_____ F_____   I do not work solely for monetary rewards.
T_____ F_____   It is okay for me to have priorities other than work.
T_____ F_____   My work reflects my values.
T_____ F_____   I live within my means and take responsibility for my financial decisions.
T_____ F_____   My spending and saving habits reflect my values and beliefs.
T_____ F_____   I balance my present-day spending with savings for the future.

Total # of True responses:_____

CULTURAL

T_____ F_____   I value the differences between people.
T_____ F_____   I am aware of my own biases and how they affect my thinking.
T_____ F_____   I look for experiences that will expose me to new ideas, people, and ways of life.

T_____ F_____ I accept that family is defined differently by different cultures.

T_____ F_____ I challenge others when they make racial or insensitive comments or jokes.

T_____ F_____ I have friends of races, cultures, or lifestyles different than my own.

T_____ F_____ I am comfortable talking with people from cultures other than my own.

T_____ F_____ I do not impose my beliefs and values on anyone.

T_____ F_____ I believe cultural diversity on a team or in a group is an asset when making decisions.

T_____ F_____ I assume good intent and ask for clarification when I don't understand what was said or implied.

Total # of True responses:_____

ENVIRONMENTAL

T_____ F_____ I consciously conserve energy (electricity, heat, light) in my home.

T_____ F_____ I recycle glass, paper, and plastic.

T_____ F_____ I limit my water use when doing dishes, bathing, or gardening.

T_____ F_____ I walk or bike when possible.

T_____ F_____ I limit the use of fertilizers and chemicals when managing my yard/outdoor living space.

T_____ F_____ I limit my consumption of meat.

T_____ F_____ I do not litter; and when I see litter, I dispose of it properly.

T_____ F_____ I take time to appreciate and spend time in nature.

T_____ F_____   I bring my own bags when shopping for groceries.

T_____ F_____   I recognize my impact on the environment and do my part to preserve it.

Total # of True responses:_____

Evaluation of Your Wellness Assessment

Step one: Using the information from your Wellness Assessment, write the name of each area in the corresponding column that represents the number of true responses. Column one – areas with 0-5 true responses, column two – areas with 6-10 true responses.

Example A: From the Wellness Assessment, person A had the following number of true responses.

Emotional – 4   Social – 5   Physical – 2   Work/Money - 9
Intellectual – 8   Cultural – 4   Spiritual – 6   Environmental – 3

Column 1 0-5 true responses	Column 2 6-10 true responses
Emotional	Work/Money
Social	Intellectual
Physical	Spiritual
Cultural	
Environmental	

Example B: From the Wellness Assessment, person B had the following number of true responses.

Emotional – 6   Social – 4   Physical – 9   Work/Money - 2
Intellectual – 7   Cultural – 3   Spiritual – 7   Environmental – 6

Column 1 0-5 true responses	Column 2 6-10 true responses
Social	Emotional
Work/Money	Physical
Cultural	Intellectual
	Spiritual
	Environmental

Evaluation of Your Wellness Assessment

Step one: Using the information from your Wellness Assessment, write the name of each area in the corresponding column that represents the number of true responses. There is no right or wrong number of true responses.

Column 1 0-5 true responses	Column 2 6-10 true responses

If all of your areas are in one column, you will be able to address them in the sequence you choose when you create your personal wellness plan.

Step Two: Complete the reflection questions that follow to determine the next steps in developing your personal wellness plan.

1. What do you notice about the results of your assessment? Is there anything that surprised you?

2. Which areas would you most like to improve?

3. What support do you need to make improvements?

Step Three: From the reflections in step two and your Wellness Assessment, create your personal wellness plan using the template that follows.

Personal Wellness Plan

Changes I want to make in my life:
Area I will work on first:

The specific change I want to make in this area is:

The specific steps I will take to make the change are:

I will know my goal has been met when:

The support systems I will put in place to ensure my success are:

Weekly Action Tracking Chart

The following chart can be used to track the specific actions from your wellness plan and the results of those actions. I also include a space for gratitude each day. The benefits of gratitude are significant, and I highly recommend you start setting a positive mindset by reflecting on the things in your life that you are grateful for each day.

Sunday	Monday	Tuesday	Wednesday	Thursday	Friday	Saturday
Gratitude:	Gratitude:	Gratitude:	Gratitude:	Gratitude:	Gratitude:	Gratitude:
Activity:	Activity:	Activity:	Activity:	Activity:	Activity:	Activity:
Result:	Result:	Result:	Result:	Result:	Result:	Result:
Sunday	Monday	Tuesday	Wednesday	Thursday	Friday	Saturday
Gratitude:	Gratitude:	Gratitude:	Gratitude:	Gratitude:	Gratitude:	Gratitude:
Activity:	Activity:	Activity:	Activity:	Activity:	Activity:	Activity:
Result:	Result:	Result:	Result:	Result:	Result:	Result:

Key Learning Points:

- Wellness enables leaders to think, act, and adapt to organizational demands and changes.
- The mind, body, and spirit are connected. To be most effective as a leader, all three must be tended to and cared for.
- Movement affects our energy, health, mind, attitude, mood, and thought processes.
- Proper nutrition, rest, and relaxation will provide the longer lasting fuel and energy necessary for optimal productivity.
- A connection with your higher source will increase confidence, focus, and strength.
- Stress can have negative or positive effects on the body. Some stress provides fuel and energy; however, too much stress can be damaging to the body and have a negative impact on health, wellness, productivity, and relationships.
- Use the six foundational components in creating your personal wellness plan.

Call for Courage

The Lunch Rush

During my sophomore year in college, I took a summer job working in a factory that made books. The first day I was there, I was working at my station and heard a bell ring. All of the workers put down whatever they were working on and hurried into the break room. I didn't know what was going on, but I followed their lead. I watched all of them open their brown lunch bags and hurriedly eat whatever snack they brought as they made small talk with each other. Exactly 12 minutes later, the next bell rang, and they closed up their bags and nearly ran back to their stations. I watched this same routine at lunch, though they got a 20-minute break, and again in the afternoon. When they needed to use the restroom, they had to wait until the foreman, George, walked by so they could ask him. I continued to watch this disturbing behavior for about a week.

I was appalled at how these really hard working people were treated. I tried to talk to them about it, and they would whisper, "Shh, don't talk about it; we'll get in trouble. It's just the way it is." I told them it wasn't right and I was going to talk to George. They were very afraid and told me not to make a fuss. I did have that talk with George, and with his 6-foot stature looming over me, I expressed how wrong it was to make these people gobble their food and have to ask permission to go to the restroom. I'm sure he hadn't experienced anyone like me before, and we got into quite a disagreement. Long story short – I got called into the main boss's office, where I was told I just needed to follow the rules and stop making trouble. I made it another few weeks, but that was the last summer I worked at that factory.

Point of Courage: advocating for injustice, speaking truth to power.

Chapter Six

LEADERSHIP DEVELOPMENT REFLECTION SYSTEM

BEING REFLECTIVE TO MOVE FORWARD

"Without reflection, we go blindly on our way, creating more unintended consequences, and failing to achieve anything useful."

– Margaret J. Wheatley

THE IDEA FOR the Leadership Development Reflection System came from two sources: my own approach to developing as a leader and a pivotal experience I had during my time as a doctoral student. From the beginning of my career, I had been of the opinion that I didn't want to be the same leader in five years as I was at that time. I wanted to learn and develop my skills so I could serve the vision of whatever organization I was in, in the best way possible. I accomplished this in two ways: by soliciting and being open to feedback from colleagues, bosses, and those whom I supervised, and by reflecting on the five core areas I focus on in this book. I thought I was doing a good job of being introspective, until I met some remarkable teachers.

Education has always been a part of my life. In the 20-year period after finishing high school, I completed a B.S. degree, followed by a M.A. degree, an additional administrative credential, and finally a doctorate. It was in this last program at the University of La Verne that I learned how powerful honest and deep introspection can be. Of all of the professors I was blessed to learn from in my school experiences, Dr. Bearley,

Dr. Larick, and Dr. McGee were the most creative, compassionate, and inspiring. From the beginning of the program, I knew I was about to embark on something special. The doctorate program they had designed was a unique balance of the theory of leadership and the practical skills needed to be a leader.

The sequence of the program was to focus on ourselves as individuals first, moving on to learning about teams and finally organizations as a whole. It was the experience of learning to look at myself with a magnifying glass that took my journey into the deepest parts of myself. Drs. Bearley, Larick, and McGee were authentic teachers who made us all feel comfortable from minute one. They connected to us and built a relationship on trust and mutual respect. By doing so, they created a safe space for me to open up to the learning they offered. We took assessments to learn about ourselves: Managing Your Energy (1996. J.E. Jones and W.L. Bearley), Effective Communication, Conflict Management, Multiple Intelligences, Emotional Intelligence, and more. I was having fun learning about myself … until we had to do a 360 assessment. In a 360 assessment, you ask your boss, colleagues, and people you supervise to complete a questionnaire about their perceptions of you as a leader. The responses are anonymous to encourage the most honest review. While my scores were positive overall, they were lower than I had anticipated. I had a choice: I could discount the ratings, believing people were just disgruntled and mean, or I could really look in my own mirror. I decided it was just like in the Wizard of Oz, time to pull back the curtain and take a look at who was behind it. That choice was my breakthrough moment.

I slowly let in that maybe I was a bull in a china shop. I probably barked more than I needed to and was quick to make judgments. I was way too serious and had hidden the lighter side of myself. I was going through the motions of being a boss and somehow forgot I was also a real human being. The person looking back at me in the mirror was someone I didn't recognize. Talk about a powerful awakening!

In the safe space created by my mentors, I began to use the tools and strategies they taught. I changed the way I approached my leadership. I approached the Leadership Development Plan they assigned with some trepidation, but with renewed enthusiasm, too. My plan included a weekly review of specific skills I wanted to learn. I increased my awareness of when I was being judgmental, communicating without compassion, and being too serious. It was the beginning of great change for me as a leader. I found a new appreciation for who I was becoming, and I know those with whom I worked did, too. I decided that I wanted to continue growing as a leader, so I made reflection a regular part of my learning. By reflecting throughout my career, including my successes and mistakes, I've been able to grow and improve, changing what doesn't work and strengthening what does.

An ongoing system of reflection is a powerful tool for leaders that connects self-awareness with developing stronger leadership skills and opportunity for greater success. Over time, I formalized my reflection process, which resulted in creating the Leadership Development Reflection System that this book is based on.

Benefits of Reflection

Reflection encourages us to develop our awareness to think more deeply to gain greater insight and learning. When we are engaged in deeper level thinking and feeling, we are more open to looking at our own authenticity, challenging who we are and how well we are walking our talk. By identifying key issues and the deeper issues underlying, we are able to challenge our current understanding of a situation. This balcony view allows us to have a more expansive comprehension that broadens our vision of possibilities. It is only in seeing our issues as an observer that we can change them.

Developing Your Leadership Skills

To develop your skills to be an effective leader, it is necessary to address the following questions: Where am I now? Where do I want to be? What do I need to do to close the gap?

Where am I now?

Having a strong sense of your values, communication style, and approach to conflict, skills in relationship building, and the status of your personal wellness is the first step to creating a strong inner foundation. The Leadership Profile at the end of this chapter will give you a snapshot of where you are in each area.

Where do I want to be?

Do you want to be a leader who is decisive, a strong and effective communicator, a good listener, effective in developing relationships, balanced in my mind, body, and spirit? Take time to envision the kind of leader you aspire to be. Is there a leader you admire that comes to mind? Be specific about the traits you want to develop.

What do I need to do to close the gap?

Refer to the assessments and tools for core values, authenticity, communication, relationships, and wellness in the preceding chapters to help you determine your gap areas.

Examples of foundational leadership skills to develop:
- Following your values in decision making
- Minimizing a specific challenge to your communication style
- Developing your listening intent—seeking to understand
- Learning to respond, rather than react, to situations
- Increase strategies to develop positive relationships
- Making yourself priority one in your personal wellness

Once you have decided on the skills you want to develop, following a growth model and creating a leadership development plan will assist you in closing the gap of where you are and where you want to be. Go slow to go fast. That is, small wins create a path to big change. Be patient in the space in the gap, between where you are and where you want to be, because it is full of possibility. It is a creative space that develops when you have one foot in the safety of what is known and the exciting prospects of the other foot reaching for growth, the unknown. I had a client who was in this space, and he was sharing how impatient he was feeling. He told me he was ready to have learned the skills he needed and thought time was passing him by. I coached him to be patient, but with a purpose. Patience doesn't mean staying static with no movement. Being patient with a purpose says you know growth is coming and are committed to the focus and practice.

Leadership Growth Action Cycle

The growth model I use when coaching and consulting with clients is:
Awareness – Education – Application – Reflection – Adjustment – Growth

Leadership Growth Action Cycle

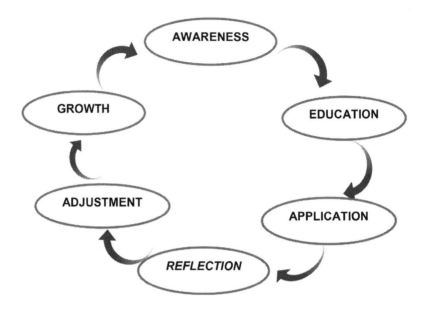

Points to Ponder on the Growth Action Cycle

Awareness – What is the issue, problem, or skill you want to develop? It is essential to spend time to fully understand the issue before rushing off to a solution. Otherwise, you may end up addressing the wrong issue, while the real one continues to cause problems. This category requires that you are honest with yourself in your reflections. Sometimes we risk being too forgiving of our weaknesses, and sometimes we risk being too critical of ourselves. Either extreme is counter-productive. Hone in on the specific items you want to address first with laser focus.

Education – What is the new skill to be learned, and what resources/tools do you need to access the new information? Is there someone in your network who can help you? Is there a class or training addressing the skills you need? Would hiring a leadership coach facilitate your development?

Application – Use the new tools and strategies you've learned and apply them to the situation you want to change.

Reflection – Reflect on the impact/success of the new learning

Adjustment – If the new skill is not addressing the behavior you wanted to change, make the needed adjustment until you get your desired result.

Growth – Anchor the new behavior by repeating it and making it part of your natural leadership style.

How I Used the Growth Action Cycle

Awareness: Every day, I found myself running from meeting to meeting, and I didn't feel prepared for any of them. Since I wasn't prepared, the meetings were not as productive as they needed to be. I was frustrated, and so were the others in the meetings.

Education: I talked with a few trusted colleagues and got ideas about things I could do to be better prepared for meetings.

Application: I applied several strategies. I organized the contents for each meeting into a separate folder. At the end of each day, I made time to look at my schedule for the following day. I went through each meeting folder that was scheduled and put them on a specific pile on my desk in the order of the time of the meeting. I also blocked out ten minutes in my schedule before each meeting to center myself and review the info in the folder.

Reflection: As long as I was disciplined and followed the strategies, I was successful. Sometimes I found that the ten minutes I had blocked out to prepare for the meeting was usurped by some urgent issue that needed my attention. In that case, because I had previewed everything the previous day, I still felt prepared.

Adjustment: The only adjustment I made was keeping my distractions during the ten minutes before a meeting to a minimum. I closed my door and didn't look at emails or pick up my phone if it rang.

Growth: The strategies became a normal part of how I structured my day.

How a Client Used the Growth Action Cycle

Awareness: The client was frustrated by staff who were not meeting project timelines.

Education: During the coaching session, we discussed each step he took with his staff when he assigned tasks. He discovered that he wasn't actually giving them a timeline. He expected them to get it done with his version of ASAP. This revelation helped him to be more explicit when giving directions.

Application: He began being more specific and stating the expected timeline.

Reflection: Staff were still not meeting the timelines to his satisfaction.

Adjustment: After further coaching, he found that he needed to add two steps to his process: 1) check for understanding—have the staff member repeat back what they heard the timeline to be, and 2) he needed to follow-up and hold the staff member accountable to the timeline.

Growth: He is successful when he applies the strategies that are now part of his regular management routine. He checks for understanding and follows up to hold staff accountable for meeting timelines.

Leadership Profile
Name_____
Date_____

My top three core values from the assessment in Chapter One:
1.
2.
3.

My behaviors and practices that reflect my values:

My primary communication style from the assessment in Chapter Three:

Strengths of my communication style:

Challenges of my communication style:

Skills I use to work effectively with other communication styles:

Skills I use to effectively address conflict:

Skills I use to build and maintain relationships:

Areas from my wellness assessment that are strong:

Areas from my wellness assessment that I want to strengthen:

Annual Reboot and Reflection

- Core Values
- Authenticity
- Communication
- Relationships
- Personal Wellness

To develop a practice of continuous improvement, I recommend an annual reflection or "reboot." Pick a time of year that works for you to reflect on your leadership skills. It could be your birthday, the beginning of the year in January, or even the end of the year in December. If you are typically extra busy during months when you have multiple celebrations, I recommend choosing another time to do your annual reflection so you are able to relax. I personally like to reflect on the day before my birthday. For me, it is a significant time because I know I will never be this age again, and looking back on the year is nostalgic and a good space to embrace the things I want to let go of and the areas of my life I want to focus on for growth.

Choose whatever day works best for you. Find a quiet place where you won't be interrupted, and begin your reflection by addressing the following situations.

Core Values and Authenticity

Review your plan from the previous year using whatever specific plan format you chose (see sample formats at the end of this chapter).

In addition to your specific plan, a few general reflections that follow may be helpful to deepen your introspection.

Situations in the past year where I applied my core values in decision making:

Situations that challenged me when applying my core values:

What I learned from applying my core values in those situations:

How have these experiences changed my values or beliefs?

What will I do differently next time based on what I've learned?

Communication and Relationships

Reflect on interactions you had with colleagues, business partners, and people you supervised.

From the interactions that were positive, what were my specific behaviors that contributed to that result?

For the interactions that were challenging or difficult, what were my specific behaviors that contributed to that result?

What will I do differently next time based on what I've learned?

Personal Wellness

What changes did I make, and how do I feel as a result of those changes?

What will I do differently next time based on what I've learned?

Congratulate Yourself!

An important part of reflection and growth is making time to take in the good of your efforts and progress. These successes are now part of your leadership foundation to build upon. In the same way you would congratulate or honor your staff, do the same for yourself. You deserve it!

Focus Areas for the Year Ahead
Core Values and Authenticity

Area of focus/change I will make:

I will know I'm successful when…

Communication and Relationships

Area of focus/change I will make:

I will know I'm successful when…

Personal Wellness

Area of focus/change I will make:

I will know I'm successful when...

Leadership Development Plan Sample Formats

Plan 1

Date:			
Competency I Want to Develop	Resources I Need to be Successful	Specific Steps to Develop the Skill	Indicators of Success
Example:	Build time into my schedule prior to the meeting	Reserve 10 minutes prior to the meeting	Positive outcome to the conversations
Centering myself before a conversation that may be difficult	Quiet area	Choose my quiet area	
		Determine the other person's communication style and the specific strategies that will increase the chance of success	

Plan 2

Changes I want to make this year:
1.
2.
3.
The specific steps I will take to make each change are:
Change #1
Change #2
Change #3
The support systems I will put in place to ensure my success are:

I will know I have been successful when:

Change #1

Change #2

Change #3

Key Learning Points:

- Reflection provides you with an opportunity to objectively replay the past year. In hindsight, you are better able to identify what works and what does not, what went right and what went wrong. It's not an opportunity to berate yourself, but to improve in the coming year.
- Being objective about your performance, actions, and decisions requires courage. Sometimes you have to be vulnerable about the past in order to be more effective in the future.
- Where do you want to be in the next three to five years? What leadership skills do you want to demonstrate and master? The answers to these questions will help you create your leadership development plan.
- The six steps in the Leadership Growth Action Cycle will help you isolate your strengths and weaknesses and provide you with the necessary information to use them as tools for improvement.

- An annual reflection is best when it covers all five of the core areas addressed in this book. Omitting any of them will result in a lack of progress and results and will leave you out of balance. Remember, as a leader, you are a whole person—your attitude, outlook, values, beliefs, communication style, relationships, and wellness all contribute to your results.

Final Thoughts

As I finish this last chapter, I am filled with hope for a bright future for all of us. When leaders are conscious and use their courage to be authentic, vulnerable, and embrace their power, organizations and communities come alive and thrive. When we get out of our own way, great things will happen. It is my hope that you open yourself and connect to the field of limitless possibilities.

You have the wisdom, tools, and courage you need to be the influential leader you are meant to be.

Use your skills, voice, and power to inspire positive change.

Thank you for being a conscious and courageous leader!

Tracy

BIBLIOGRAPHY

Alessandra, Tony Ph.D. and O'Connor, Michael J. PH.D. *The Platinum Rule*. New York: Warner Books, Inc., 1996.

Arrendondo, Lani. *Communicating Effectively*. New York: McGraw-Hill, 2000.

Bolton, Robert and Bolton, Dorothy Grover. *People Styles at Work*. New York: Amacom, 1996.

Cashman, Kevin. *Leadership from the Inside Out*. Provo, Utah: Executive Excellence Publishing, 2001.

Dethmer, Jim, Chapman, Diana, Warner-Klemp, Kaley. *The 15 Commitments of Conscious Leadership*. San Bernardino, 2014.

Cloke, Kenneth and Goldsmith, Joan. *Resolving Conflicts at Work*. San Francisco, 2000.

Dweck, Carol S. Ph.D. *Mindset*. New York: Ballantine, 2008.

Goleman, Daniel. *Focus*. New York: Harper Collins, 2013.

Ledwell, Natalie. Ultimate Success Masterclass. Web-based class. 2013

Moxley, Russ S. *Leadership and Spirit*. San Francisco: Jossey-Bass, 2000.

Senge, Peter et.al. *The 5th Discipline Fieldbook*. New York: Bantam Doubleday Dell Publishing, 1994.

Smith, Hyrum W. *The Power of Living Your Values*. New York: Fireside, 2000.

Travis, John M.D., Ryan, Regina Sara. *The Wellness Workbook 3rd edition*. New York: Ten Speed Press, 2004.

Weisinger, Hendrie Ph.D. *Emotional Intelligence at Work*. San Francisco: Jossey-Bass, 1998.

ABOUT THE AUTHOR

Dr. Tracy Tomasky

Dr. Tracy Tomasky believes that *everyone* has the ability to lead. As a leadership coach in her own company, she works with individuals, businesses, and organizations to enhance those abilities and develop approaches to leadership that make a long-lasting impact. She is committed to helping her clients discover their courage to lead with integrity, authenticity, and a strong connection to their team.

Throughout her 30+ year career as a key executive in business and education, Tracy learned firsthand that successful leadership relies on successful relationships. As a valued education director, she expertly led a large school district department serving 4,200 children and families for more than 10 years. She has served in leadership roles for local, statewide, and national organizations and board associations.

Tracy believes that the most effective leaders are driven by their core values, and she is currently demonstrating that in her commitment to social justice work as a volunteer with several organizations throughout Northern California.

Dr. Tracy Tomasky holds an Ed.D. in Organizational Leadership and an M.A. in Educational Administration. To learn more about her work, please visit: www.tracytomasky.com.

Made in the USA
Columbia, SC
20 August 2020